CW00373541

History, People and Places in Brittany

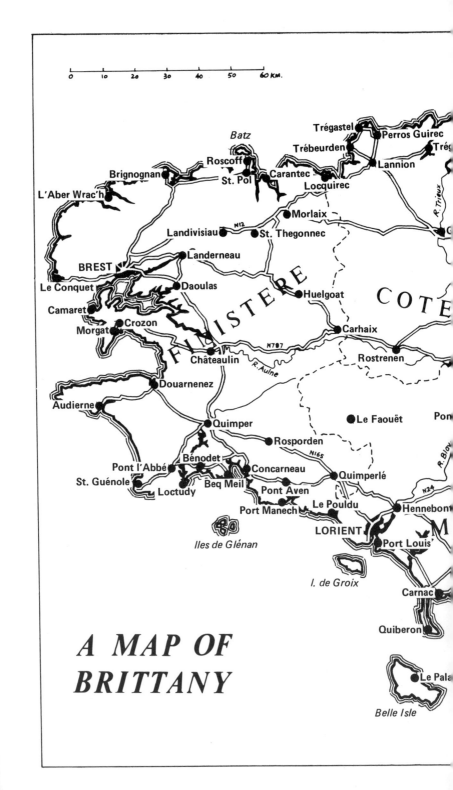

A MAP OF
BRITTANY

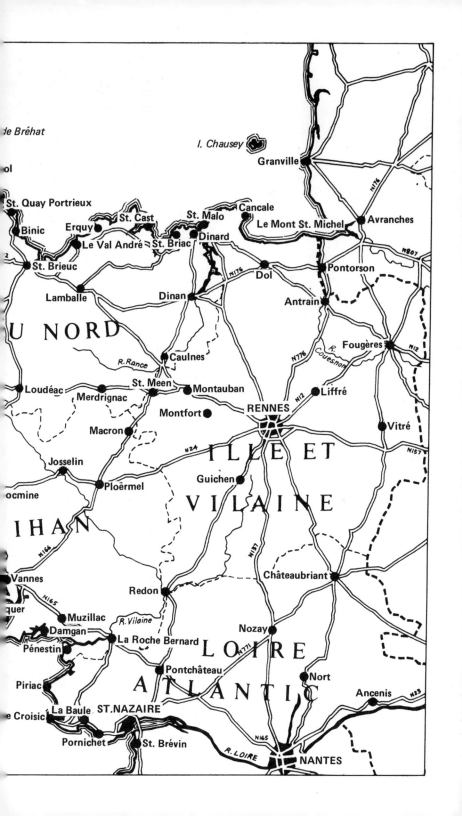

Rennes

History, People and Places in

Brittany

by Neil Lands

SPURBOOKS LIMITED

Published by Spurbooks Limited
6 Parade Court, Bourne End, Buckinghamshire

ISBN 0 904978 26 5

Other titles in this series include:

Normandy
The Dordogne
Beyond the Dordogne
Provence
Languedoc-Roussillon
Burgundy
Auvergne
Northern France – *Picardy & Artois*

The Cotswolds
Lake District
Dorset
Western Highlands
East Sussex
West Sussex
Yorkshire

Forthcoming titles:
Eastern France – *Alsace, Lorraine*

Designed and produced by
Mechanick Exercises, London

Typesetting by Inforum, Portsmouth

Printed in Great Britain by
Tonbridge Printers Limited
Peach Hall Works, Tonbridge, Kent

THIS BOOK IS FOR JOHN ANTOINE

Acknowledgements

The author and publisher would like to thank Pauline Hallam of the French Government Tourist Office; Toby Oliver of Brittany Ferries; The Syndicats of Rennes, Vitré, Nantes, Fougères, and St Malo; Elfie Tran; and John Antoine, for their help with this book. The endpaper map is by Terry Brown, and the manuscript preparation was undertaken by Estelle Huxley and Mary Powell. All photographs are by the author.

Contents

Illustrations

1
Brittany: An Historical Introduction

If you should find yourself in Dinan and climb up the narrow path which leads towards the ramparts from the River Rance you will come eventually to the little park known as the English Garden.

Here, well concealed in the trees, stands the church of St Sauveur, and in a little chapel in the north aisle, a large stone slab bearing the curious inscription, which if translated, reads roughly as follows:

> *Here lies the heart of Messire Bertrand Duguesclin sometime Constable of France who died on the 13th day of July 1380, and whose body lies with the Kings at St Denis in France.*

In *France*, you will note. Elsewhere! Brittany, where we now stand, is, or was, therefore, somewhere apart from France, a separate country. This fact, if taken at face value can come as a considerable blow to any devoted Francophile for Francophilia is an infection to which even the French are not immune and one for which the only cure is more of the ailment.

So, if Brittany is not France, should we even go there? Will it have what we seek and supply our wants in food, wine and ambiance? The answer, happily, is a firm 'yes' and no lover of France can fail to be charmed by this delightful province.

Brittany is big. Today, strictly speaking, it embraces four *départements*, but we should still include the recently excised Loire-Atlantique which brings the true total to five, the other four

13

being Finistère, Morbihan, Ille-et-Vilaine, and lastly the Côtes du Nord, where our travels will begin, along the coast.

Brittany is famous for its coast. There are over seven hundred miles of it, a stretch embracing wide sandy beaches, rocky headlands, tall cliffs, innumerable islands, little coves, salt marsh and fen. We will tour all around this coast, but you should go inland as well, to the '*Argoat*', the 'country of wood', to give your travels variety as well as history. A traveller who sticks to the coast would miss a great deal.

Brittany has a long history and one where the origins are truly 'wrapped in the mists of time', shrouded with legend, folklore and superstition. You will find it difficult to divide historical fact from ancient legend, and since it is all interesting you need not try too hard. Brittany is still mysterious and for many centuries was not even 'Brittany' at all. It is, at heart, a Celtic country, and they came before the Gauls. Who these early people were, the people who built the megaliths of Finistère and erected the menhirs at Carnac, we do not really know. We know that they were succeeded by the Gauls who were divided, as elsewhere, into the various clans of that complex federation and they called their land Armorica, '*the land facing the sea*'.

In 56 B.C. the Romans came, the legions of Caesar, to conquer and subdue the tribes and those who would not sumbit, like the Venetii, were slaughtered, or sold into slavery. The Roman rule was relatively brief and at this tip of their Empire, less uniform than elsewhere, and the tribal names for one, have often been preserved. The Venetii were from what is now Vannes, the Redones came from Rennes, the Namnetes from Nantes and so on.

Cassius and Brutus conquered Armorica for Caesar, the one by land and the other by sea, Brutus destroying the Venetii fleet in the Gulf of Morbihan and, for the next four hundred years the Roman rule remained, before it in turn crumbled under the coming of the Northmen. By this time though, the country was already Christian. Pagan religions and the Druidic rites were swept away by the eloquence of a host of saints from Ireland and Wales, those Celtic saints with unusual names, who made their way to Brittany, not just in boats but on leaves, or floating stones, (or so we are told!)

As the first centuries of the Christian era wore on, this trickle of missionaries was vastly increased by refugees, as the Saxons began to smother first the outlying settlements in Ireland and then the

14

Tour L'Horloge, Dinan

coasts of Britain, forcing those who lived there to flee abroad.

'If there were a hundred tongues in every head' wrote one monk at the time, *'they could not tell all we have endured from those valiant, wrathful, purely pagan people'*.

The Saxons, in short, stove in the walls of the Roman Empire, and by the middle of the 5th century they were established in Britain and had either extinguished the Romano-Britons or forced them to flee. The people of Britain had to go somewhere, and, as their land had been taken by the Saxons, so they resolved to conquer others in their turn.

About the year 400 A.D., Maximus, a Roman-British general, *'fitted out a great fleet and filled it with every armed warrior in Britain and went into the land that is called Armorica and made war upon the Gauls that lived there'*.

This is the basis of the story on how the Britons came to Brittany, and it is probably untrue. Western Armorica had been peacefully infiltrated by the Britons for centuries and any 'invasion' was probably no more than the arrival of troops evacuated from outlying garrisons. However, this period saw the end of Armorica and the land came to be called *'Brittany'* — the 'little Britain'.

The Saxons soon followed, of course, but here they were resisted. The Britons, or perhaps we should now call them Bretons, really had nowhere else to go. The rest of what is now France was also under attack from the Teutonic Franks and the Visigoths, but even as they settled in the country to the east and south, the Bretons became established in Brittany until, by the middle of the 6th century, their grip on the province was secure.

The earliest historian of the Franks was Gregory of Tours, and he relates how, in his time, at about the end of the 6th century, Brittany contained three 'Kingdoms' which warred against the Franks and each other. The Frankish King, Clovis, defeated the Bretons and, in Frankish terms, replaced their 'Kingdoms' with 'Counties'. Each Count continued to behave as a King however, and refused to either acknowledge Frankish authority or pay taxes, and the early Merovingians were content to leave well alone.

Charlemagne sent his paladin Roland to Brittany on a punitive expedition in 778, and in the following century, the Emperor, Louis the Pious, gave his Imperial support to the Count of Vannes, Nöminoe, who defeated his rivals, conquered the entire province and held it as a subject king. After Louis' death though, Nöminoe threw off all his allegiance to the Carolingians, and his successors, the Kings of Brittany, fought the Franks and the Northmen for the next two hundred years.

In 939 the Breton Alain Barbe-Torte defeated the Normans and Alain's descendants ruled Brittany as a quasi-independent state until 1488, paying little more than lip service to the King of France. At the end of this period during the Hundred Years War, Brittany was scourged by the War of the Breton Succession, when the rival houses of Blois and Montfort fought for the province and were supported, in hopes of allegiance by the Kings of France and England.

We ought to look at this business of fuedalism. The fuedal system is best regarded as a pyramid, the king at the top, linked by an interlocking series of allegiances to the peasant at the bottom. It was a system held together by self-interest. The lord promised protection and the subject promised obedience and loyalty.

However, in practice, there were many exceptions. The kings of France were, in theory, the overlords of all France, and every lord owed the king his obedience. In practice such nobles as the Dukes of Brittany, Aquitaine and Burgundy and the Counts of Toulouse were independent sovereigns, who swore an oath of homage to the king on their accession and otherwise did exactly as they pleased. During the Middle Ages the king slowly destroyed these over-mighty subjects, and brought the entire Kingdom under his actual, as opposed to his theoretical, rule. The Counts of Toulouse were extirpated by the Albigensian Crusade in the 13th century. The Dukes of Aquitaine, who were usually also the Kings of England, were eventually defeated and dispersed, and the Dukes of Burgundy, after a hundred years of glory, had conveniently died. By the end of the 15th century, only Brittany still held out as an independent power and a combination of force and marriage was to bring the Duchy down.

* * *

You will not go far in Brittany before you see somewhere or something named after 'La Duchesse Anne', the last reigning sovereign of an independent Brittany.

As part of the treaty following a rebellion, Duke Francis II had promised that his children should not be married without the permission of the French King, but when he died in 1488, his daughter, Anne, married Maximillian of Austria by proxy. Maximillian had previously been married to Mary, daughter of the last Duke of Burgundy, Charles the Bold. The French King, Charles VIII, had no intention of being encircled by the House of Hapsburg, and marched an army into Brittany.

Just to complicate matters, Charles was at the time betrothed to Maximillian's daughter, Margaret, but in the end, all betrothals, marriages and arrangements were annulled and Charles VIII of France married the Duchesse Anne of Brittany and much to everyone's surprise, including I suspect, their own, they were very happy.

Then, in 1499, Charles banged his head on a lintel in the château at Amboise and suddenly died. What followed is an intriguing example of medieval manoeuvres, and so brace yourself for another whirl on the medieval marriage-go-round.

All Anne's children by Charles had died, and the heir to the throne was Louis, Duke of Orléans, a friend of her father, who was crowned as Louis XII. Louis was already married, but he, like

The Arms of Anne of Brittany

Charles VIII, had no wish to lose control over the Breton duchy, and begged the Borgia Pope, Alexander VI, for an annulment, which was brought to Chinon by no less a person that Cesare Borgia himself, who obtained in return the services of a French army. The annulment obtained, Louis then married his predecessor's widow!

In 1499 their daughter, Claude of France, was born and she was swiftly betrothed, at six years of age, to the heir to the throne, Francois d'Angoulême, the future Francis I. Anne's marriage agreement with Louis stated that Brittany would remain independent, but after Anne's death in 1514, the king prevailed on Claude to ignore this provision and bequeath the Duchy to the Dauphin Francis, before she in turn died in 1524.

Francis I then persuaded the *parlement* of Brittany that their best long-term interests lay in union with France and in 1532, they met at Vannes and requested the Royal favour, which was gleefully granted by the King at Nantes later the same year. And phew! you may think, thank goodness for that. Not all Bretons would agree with you.

Brittany survived the ravages of the Hundred Years' War, the Wars of Religion and the Revolution better than most, but fell on rather harder times after the establishment of the Republic. A Civil War against the Royalist, Catholic Bretons, or the *Chouans*, as they came to be called, raged in Brittany and the Vendée for many years, and the period was marked by many atrocities, notably the mass executions of Royalists at Rennes and Nantes, where thousands were tied together and thrown into the Loire to drown.

In 1532 though, the French Crown had gained a formidable inheritance, a huge tract of land, a wolf's head snarling into the Atlantic, and lordship over a tough race of people, good soldiers and great seamen.

* * *

Inland, Brittany is a rather uniform country of rolling hills and valleys, not mountainous, but never monotonous. Only in the Arrée 'mountains' which sheltered the frontier of Finistère, are they any high hills and, apart from the Loire, there are few big rivers, but many creeks and inlets. The word that comes to mind again and again in Brittany is 'agreeable'. It really is, on all levels, very agreeable, and in many ways unique.

19

A bay on the Côtes du Nord

The Breton tongue is still spoken, although mainly by older people, and the country has a tradition and a folklore quite divorced from that of France. Apart from the départements, and the difference between the '*Armour*', the coast, and the '*Argoat*', the hinterland, the country is also divided into 'Upper' and 'Lower' Brittany.

'Upper' Brittany lies inland to the east, and just to be awkward is in fact much less hilly than 'Lower' Brittany, which lies roughly west of a line between Vannes and St Brieuc. Breton is mostly spoken in 'Lower' Brittany, away from the language polluting frontier with France, and it is here also that you will see more than elsewhere those lacey Breton *coiffes*. The *coiffes* are a feature of Breton dress and they come in a variety of shapes, of which the tall *Bigouden* one is most familiar. These Breton costumes, like the language, are slowly dying out, and can now be seen only on the old people at the fairs and market days, sometimes at weddings and, as a matter of custom and respect at the Breton 'pardons'.

20

A 'pardon' is a procession, a pilgrimage, and nearly every Breton town has an annual pardon to the tomb of the local saint. The Bretons are a religious people, and you will find their churches well preserved, full of curiosities and surprisingly large.

Their religious architecture also contains those surprising manifestations of religious fervour, the calvaries. These, often used to typify Brittany, are in fact quite rare, and found mainly in Finistère, where they form the centrepiece in that other artistic phenomenon, the 'parish close'.

Breton churches are also notable for fine steeples, belfries and bell towers, and from a host of opportunities I have selected some of the best for us to visit. I should explain that here, as in my other books, while this book covers the entire province, I have made no attempt to visit every town or village. There are still plenty of places for you to discover on your own, where, with any luck, *'the (other) tourists don't go'*, but I have, I believe, included the best.

Quite apart from religion, but strongly linked with it in the past, is folklore. Brittany is the home of Sir Lancelot, of Morgan le Fay and the Lady of the Lake, of Druids, of wishing wells and magic fountains. We will visit Brocéliande, and the haunts of Merlin and you will find, especially in the stories of the saints that in Brittany fact, legend and superstition are inextricably mixed. Brittany contains the largest number of megalithic remains in Western Europe, notably at Carnac, and in the north of Finistère, so that lovers of pre-history will find their passions fully indulged, but Brittany, the land of Armorica, remains the country of the sea.

* * *

People will tell you, by way of description, that Brittany is very like Cornwall, a land of cliffs and inlets, and all this is very true. The entire coast is seamed with creeks and harbours, so that fishing, next to tourism, is the major industry. The yachtsman has now ousted the fisherman from many of his old haunts, and every tidal water now supports a flotilla of pleasure craft, which crowd these attractive, if dangerous, waters. Benodet, in the south of Finistère is just one of a hundred yachting centres, but one we will visit as an example of the best.

Apart from modern pleasures, the country has ancient charms. Some of the towns, Dinan, Vannes, Vitré, for example are medieval

Calvary at Playben

gems, still full of old leaning buildings hovering over narrow cobbled streets. Others, equally ancient, were ravaged by bombing in the late war and have been rebuilt with some taste but little imagination. St Nazaire, Brest and Lorient are good examples of this. The largest city in the province is Nantes; even though Nantes is now part of the neighbouring province, Pays de La Loire, it remains a large attractive Breton city of considerable charm, and we will enjoy our visit there.

If you like castles, and I confess myself an addict, you should not fail to visit Vitré, Fougères, Josselin, or the later Vauban fortress of Port Louis opposite Lorient. These still have their medieval or seventeenth century walls intact and are well preserved mighty castles, which would be fortresses even today. If your pleasure lies more at the table than in furious war, then you will be well served in Brittany, *provided* you like sea food.

The seas around the coast are, in every sense, bountiful. The lobsters of Camaret lead a whole procession of crabs, langoustines, oysters, mussels, whelks and winkles on to your plate, all served in a variety of ways and all accompanied by the only Breton wine, Muscadet, unless perhaps by cider. I have rarely eaten as well anywhere as I have in Brittany and never found a region where the standard of cooking was so consistently high and the cost of good eating so reasonable.

As to the weather, well, it rains. Not to excess, but regularly. If the weather in Britain is wet, then you would be advised to head for the southern shore and enjoy the Morbihan, while, if the summer in Britain is warm, then the North Coast of Brittany, the Côte d'Emeraude, has much to recommend it.

Brittany is popular with holidaymakers and you should try and visit it out of season, away from the peak period mid-July to early September. If you *must* go at that time, then you will need to book ahead, especially if travelling through the very popular regions. Personally, I find Brittany attractive out of season, in May or June and during the month of October. The province is a paradise for birds, and therefore for birdwatchers, and these are the months when the great flocks of seabirds can be seen at their best.

In this book I have tried to seek out the lesser known places and would urge you to do the same, following always the 'Three Principles for Happy Travelling in France', which are to travel on minor roads, to stay in Logis de France hotels, and to eat from the Michelin guide. If you do that, you won't go very far wrong. Good maps are always useful and the whole region is covered in the Institut Geographique National Carte Touristique 1:250,000 No. 5 *Bretagne*. I also rely, for good eating and decent hotels, on the Gault-Millau *Guide de la France*, and those places where I had a particularly good meal have been mentioned in this book.

* * *

So much then for the history and the places. There is plenty to see and do in Brittany so I have no fears for your enjoyment, but what of the people.

St Malo, which we will visit first, the terminal port of Brittany Ferries, is said to have produced more famous sons than any other town in France.

Brittany has a score of notable names to look back on, from knights like Bertrand Duguesclin, who harried the English up and down France, to explorers and navigators like Cartier and Surcouf, to soldiers like Cambronne, writers like Châteaubriand and Jules Verne, and lovers like Abélard. All were Bretons, and proud of it.

As we travel round this large and agreeable province we will find many traces of these people and their past, for the Bretons' instinct is to preserve their history and traditions and resist the new, if newness is all that it has to recommend it. Brittany is a French province, but one with its own distinct and special flavour. It is very like certain parts of England, and it takes a while for the traveller to absorb that exciting 'foreign' feeling, but, be sure, it will arrive.

If I look up from writing this and look through my window, I see the grey skies and dripping trees of an English winter, but I can still see, in my mind, the white houses, the vivid green seas and the high blue skies of Brittany. Why are we waiting here then— let us begin.

2
The Côtes du Nord: St Malo to St Brieuc

St Malo, city of corsairs! Coming in from the sea, even the sea-scape of St Malo is distinctly menacing. The ship weaves its way carefully through a maze of rocks and reefs, threading a course from light-house to lighthouse. Coming in at night, the approach is made through a network of flashing red, green and white lights, all over-towered by the regular glare from the lighthouse on the height of Cap Fréhel.

From earliest times until the end of the Napoleonic Wars, these reefs were the first bastion protecting the raiding craft of St Malo from summary justice at the hands of the British Navy. During the 16th and 17 centuries in particular, few vessels in the Channel could escape paying tribute to the privateers who sailed from St Malo and took their ships and plunder home again to a safe harbour in the Rance, under the guns of St Malo and the Tour Solidor.

As you sail in, the town itself, St Malo *Inter Muros*, lies snugly to your left, behind high ramparts. It looks the archetypal Vauban fortress, but this appearance is in some ways deceptive.

The old fortress-town and port of St Malo was obliterated in the last war, when after the Normany invasion of 1944 the German commander withdrew inside the walls and defied the American Army to evict him.

The siege of St Malo lasted two weeks, during which time the fortress was pounded by field artillery and the guns of the Fleet. When the Germans eventually surrendered, old St Malo was a wreck.

However, the *Malouins*, the people of St Malo, are a tough,

The coast off St Malo

resilient crowd and they decided to rebuild their city in the old style, so what you see on arrival is a reconstructed medieval-to-18th-century city with the more useful 20th-century additions of decent lighting, smooth streets and mains drainage, to make your stay more pleasant.

The port is busy and the fishing fleet sails, as always, for the cod-banks off Iceland. The sea is the true market for St Malo and many great French seamen have sailed from under her walls.

In the 16th century, Jacques Cartier sailed to Newfoundland, but discovered instead the wide estuary of the great St Lawrence. Cartier thought he had arrived, like Marco Polo, in Cathay, rather than America, but when he met Indians along the river, he took their name for the word 'village' — *Canada* — to be the name of their country and possessed the land for the French King, a step which eventually led to conflict and the Seven Years War with England.

Another great colonizer from St Malo was Mahé La Bourdon-

26

St Malo in a gale

nais, who explored the Indies, but a more warlike and tragic figure was Porcon de la Bardinais, who commanded a St Malo frigate guarding French shipping against the Barbary pirates, but was captured and taken to Algiers.

He would normally have been sent to row out his life on the galleys, but the Bey of Algiers sent him to Louis XIV with peace proposals, charging him to return to imprisonment if the proposals were rejected. They were, and in blunt terms, but Porcon kept his word and carried the King's harsh answer back to Algiers, where it so enraged the Bey that he had Porcon blown to pieces at the cannon's mouth. A sticky end was the frequent fate of St Malo's sailors, for they were inveterate pirates, and even the King's commission or *letters of marque* could not always convince their captors that their aims were legitimate.

From St Malo sailed a host of pirates, privateers, navigators and corsairs, the difference between each category being rather obscure, especially to their victims. Their lust for plunder and adven-

27

ture took them far afield. Surcouf, for example, ravaged the East India Company's ships on the trade routes to the Indies, and did so well by it that he retired a rich man before he was forty.

A hundred years before Surcouf, between 1673 and 1736, René Duguay-Trouin, harassed the Channel shipping and landed men to raid the coast of England. These men and a host of others lived from the sea and enriched the city from their spoils. They are commemorated at the town's museum at the St Vincent Gate.

You can get a taste of a vanished but more recent *Malouin* way of life if you call in for a drink at the *Hotel Univers* on the Place Châteaubriand, where the bar is decorated with paintings, ship's models, and old photographs, all recording the great days of St Malo and the sea, in times more peaceful than those of the corsairs.

* * *

The *Inter-Muros* is completely encircled by the repaired 12th-century ramparts, buttressed here and there with towers and *glacis*, decorated with statues of the town's great men and with fine views over the sea approaches. If you look down into the streets you can also see, under the walls, some of the town's fine restaurants, notably *La Duchesse Anne,* the *Central* in the Grande Rue where you will get a very warm welcome, or the *Auberge de l'Hermine*.

Moving round the ramparts you will come eventually to Beaufils' statue of Châteaubriand, another son of St Malo, who was almost born on the little islet, Le Grand Bé, which lies just off the port, in September 1768. His mother, who must have become bored with waiting, had decided to go for a row in a small boat. She went into labour when they arrived at Le Grand Bé, so the party hurriedly returned to St Malo and René was born within a few hours.

René de Châteaubriand spent most of his boyhood in St Malo, went to school in Dinan, and at other times lived with his parents in their gloomy château at Combourg. The family, although noble, were not over-blessed with money, and in an effort to restore their fortunes, his father took up ship-owning, the only occupation open to a gentleman under the Ancien Régime which did not involve the loss of his patent of nobility. The venture was reasonably successful, and his son enjoyed the benefits of an expensive education.

René tried various careers, including the army and diplomacy,

Museum and Town Hall, St Malo.

but he began to write at twenty-two, an occupation which gradually overtook everything else and he continued to do so until his death at eighty.

The French often refer to Châteaubriand as their greatest writer, mainly on account of his style, and this is charitable from the nation that has produced Hugo, Zola, Balzac, and Voltaire, to name but a few; especially so since Châteaubriand's style is, in the main, gloomy. His major work, *Memoires d'Outre-Tombe*, 'Memories from Beyond the Grave' is a typical example. This can probably be accounted for by the fact that his private life was largely unhappy.

His childhood was depressing, his marriage disasterous, his ambition consuming. He was not a happy man. At the end of his life he asked the people of St Malo for "six feet of rock" on the Grand Bé, and there, on the island where he was so very nearly born, he was buried in 1848.

St Malo has now long outgrown the walls and is a well-developed holiday resort. Most of the hotels are in the suburb of Paramé, to the east, and I particularly recommend the *Hôtel Alba* in the Rue des Dunes, which overlooks the bay. One wild night there I was awoken by the spray from waves breaking over the quay and slashing against the windows, and opened them up to receive a thorough drenching. Further down the coast lies Cancale, where the oysters come from, of which more later.

St Malo today is a cheerful bustling place and, like most seaports, an exciting place to visit. It has an aquarium with a host of Channel fish, some of quite alarming aspect, a fine museum in the old Castle with relics of the corsairs, and numerous walks about the town to the forts and, at low tide, across the causeway to Le Grand Bé. Châteaubriand's tomb, under a massive granite cross, is the seaward side, looking out to the ocean, and away from the little town which, as Châteaubriand remarked, had as fine a record for famous men as any town in France.

* * *

Opposite St Malo lies Dinard, a complete contrast; quiet, elegant, almost refined. You can reach Dinard from St Malo by the cross-harbour ferry and you step ashore to a different world. Were the term not a touch vulgar, Dinard could describe itself as the 'Pearl of the Côte d'Emeraude', for Dinard, let it be said, has style.

René de Châteaubriand, Combourg.

Tour Solidor, on the Rance

When just a little port, it was 'discovered' by the British and Americans in about 1870. They came first to visit, and then to settle there, and these strangers set their mark on the former port and it remains after much building and re-building, Edwardian in aspect and extremely popular. We had toured it for only a short time when my companion described it with a succinct, "Torquay", which from the walk around the Pointe de Moulinet it greatly resembles.

Dinard has large hotels, a casino, excellent beaches, a huge indoor swimming pool, built at vast cost some twenty years ago, and some excellent and expensive restaurants, notably the *Roche-Corneille* and, more typically and less costly, the quaintly-named *Petit Robinson*. Dinard, I confess it, has panache. In summer it is thronged with a lively and well-dressed crowd and it reminded me, rather achingly, of long ago childhood holidays in Devon, of sand and rock pools, of walks along the cliffs, and of fishing nets and seaweed, chasing crabs and endless hours spend trying to prise shellfish off the rocks. Nostalgia isn't what it was, so somewhat depressed I took the ferry back to St Malo and headed south for the Tour Solidor and Dinan.

On the right bank of the Rance, down across the estuary, you will see the high bulk of the Tour Solidor, built by Jean IV in 1382 to overawe the *Malouins*, a vain task one imagines, in view of their intransigent reputation. It now contains the *Musée des Cap-Horners*, dedicated to the days of the clipper ships and a most interesting place to visit, while the *Hôtel de la Rance* nearby is a good place for lunch.

* * *

A guidebook should be positive. My favourite town in the Côtes du Nord is Dinan. Wherever else you go, go there. But then, I like old towns, red flowers against golden walls, battlements and leaning houses, and Dinan has all of that and more. You could happily spend days in Dinan, exploring the town on foot, or foraying out into the nearby countryside, but head first for the main Square, the Place du Guesclin and have a *kir* at a table outside the *Hôtel Avaugour*. To be exact, the *Avaugour* is in the Place du Champ-Clos, of which more anon, but the difference is infinitesimal since the two are only separated by a low wall.

C

Dinan is the home-town of the good knight, Bertrand Duguesclin, Fabian General and sometime Constable of France. You will see his equestrian statue from your seat outside the *Avaugour*, and a fine statue it is, though closer inspection will show you that whatever his personal and military qualities, Bertrand was not overburdened with good looks. He was, in fact, downright ugly.

Bertrand was born at La Motte Broom castle, north of Dinan, then a possession of the Duke Jean III. He was knighted in 1356, the year of Poitiers, and entered the French King's service at a time when the King himself was a captive in England. Meanwhile, the War of the Breton Succession was raging and in 1359 Duguesclin occupied Dinan with a small force and held it against an English army under John, Duke of Lancaster. During the siege, Bertrand was challenged to single combat by an English knight, Sir Thomas Canterbury, and promptly accepted. The combat took place between the armies, in what is now the Champ-Clos, and Canterbury was left dead upon the field. Dead, but not entirely forgotten; there is a *Canterbury Restaurant* just opposite the Champ-Clos in the Rue Ste Clair, and the food at least is memorable.

Duguesclin fought the English for the next sixteen years, and he was not always so successful. He was captured at Auray and, ransomed, captured again at the Battle of Najera in Spain, and yet again at Juigne, but in the end Duguesclin's Fabian tactics wore the English down.

Duguesclin liked the English, and always enjoyed his periods of captivity in the English Court, for he was never kept in prison.

Many of the English knights, notably John Chandos and Robert Knollys, were his personal friends, and Duguesclin just wanted the English to stay on their own side of the Channel, a widely-shared sentiment at the time, and indeed later.

For their part, the English admired Bertrand immensely and took a great interest in his welfare. When he was unhorsed at Auray and in danger of death, John Chandos rode to his rescue through the press and persuaded him to surrender his sword, saying: *"Come now, Bertrand, give up your sword. This day cannot be yours, but there will, certes, be another"*.

Bertrand's wife, the beautiful and mysterious Tiphanie, who was said to have second sight, and might, but for Bertrand's reputation, been burned as a witch, also came from Dinan, and when Bertrand himself was dying outside the walls of Châteauneuf, he expressed

Bertrand Duguesclin, Dinan

Dinan centre

the wish to return to his home on the Rance, the town of his boyhood.

*　*　*

Dinan is a walled town of some 20,000 inhabitants, built above the Rance. After your *apéritif*, leave the Champ-Clos and make your way to the old Keralty maison in the Rue Léhon. This is a fine 16th-century house, which now contains the *Syndicat d'Initiative*. They will provide you with a variety of information and a map of the town and following this will take you to all the sights. There is a

Rue Jerzual, Dinan

music school beside the **Maison** Keralty, and we departed on our tour to a long and well-played fanfare on a trumpet!

The Tour d l'Horloge, which lies just ahead, was presented to the town by Duchesse Anne in 1507 and overlooks the *Vieille Ville*, the old *bourg*. The centre, the Place des Merciers has 15th-century houses leaning wearily towards each other, and from here you turn down the steep and beautiful Rue du Jerzual, which alone would make a trip to Brittany worthwhile.

The houses along the Rue Jerzual date from the 16th century and are beautifully preserved. Window-boxes crammed with geraniums crowd every ledge, while the lucky occupants are mainly artists, engaged in pottery, weaving, ironwork, painting or sculpture. This street leads down steeply to the encircling walls and the Rue du Petit Ford. Dinan also was a port, and the banks of the Rance at the Vieux-Pont are overlooked by a high viaduct. A footpath leads up from the viaduct to the so-called 'English Garden' behind the basilique of St Sauveur, which contains, as we have seen in Chapter 1, the heart of Duguesclin who died of fever in 1380 while besieging Châteauneuf-de-Randon in the Midi. The body went to St Denis, but his heart, in death as in life, belonged to Dinan. The basilique was built about 1120 in a mixture of styles, and has some fine glass and sculpture, as well as a curious monument to St Roch who freed the town from plague in the 16th century. The windows will interest saint-spotters, for they show the saints being martyred and the trades of which they are now the patrons.

Wandering around the town you will pass the school where Châteaubriand was educated and arrive at the great château, now a museum of Breton dress, on the south-west rampart. Palm trees flourish in the old moat, a sign of how mild is the climate, and the fortress itself is well worth a visit, as indeed are the old walls.

The castle was built rapidly between 1382 and 1387. Oliver de Clisson was based here and scourged the country with his *routiers*, and the Duchesse Anne herself sheltered here in 1507, giving the town the Tour Horloge in thanks for its hospitality.

In 1446, Gilles, the younger son of Duke Jean was imprisoned in the castle dungeon, apparently for arguing with his brother Duke François! It must have been a considerable quarrel, because after being starved and beaten, the young prince was finally strangled by his jailors. The castle is well preserved and an excellent example of a late medieval fortress.

Château at Dinan

On the other side of the town lies the Cloitre des Cordeliers, another building with a grisly tale to tell. Jean de Montfort, who after Auray became Duke Jean IV, visited the town in 1378 and found to his rage that the Franciscan monks of les Cordeliers still had a portrait of his dead rival, their patron Charles of Blois, on the wall. He ordered it to be removed, but when the monks did so, the wall behind it began to bleed, a spectacle which horrified the Duke so much that he fled hysterically from the town.

* * *

To leave Dinan more peacefully and make a pleasant excursion, you can descend any morning to the old port on the Rance and take one of the motor-boats which ply up the river between St Malo and Dinan — a trip of about two hours.

This is far the best way to see the Rance, for no road directly overlooks it. The river winds along the steep wooded valley, gradually widening as it nears the grand *barrage*. This is not just a dam, but a tidal power station. When the tide flows in, the turbines turn. When the tide retreats, the pent-up waters behind the dam pour out after it, and so the turbines turn again. It is as close to perpetual motion as the world has yet devised, and is open to visitors with a mechanical bent!

The boat will take you back to Dinan, the junction for all the roads in this part of the Duchy, and from Dinan you can tour out in all directions, either on foot, for this is great walking country, or by car.

Léhon, a suburb of Dinan, is famous locally for its cloister and for the calvary of St Esprit, erected in 1359 by John of Gaunt, Duke of Lancaster, whose troops were besieging the town. The cloister is also the mausoleum of the Beaumanoir family, an ancient Breton stock. This stands on the remains of a chapel built by Nöminoe, the first King of Brittany. You can walk to Léhon from Dinan, past the viaduct over the Rance, an ideal evening stroll.

To the south, within the Côtes du Nord, the département with which we are presently concerned, lies the fortress of Caradeuc. Again and again in Brittany you will discover that the fortresses lie in the periphery of regions, designed to defend rather than oppress the inhabitants, and so it is here, although the present buildings are not particularly old.

Caraduec, twenty kilometres south of Dinan, was built on an ancient site and dominates the road to Rennes. The present château was built about 1776 by Louis-René de Chalotais, who, as Procurer of Rennes defended the rights of the Breton *parlement* against the ever-encroaching central power of Paris. Nearby lies the village of Bécherel, a walled little place of considerable charm, with great wide views north towards Dinan. East of Bécherel, lies Tinteniac, a village full of flowers, while to the west of Bécherel, past Jugon which has the oldest church in Brittany and a castle, it is as well to press on west to the old Penthièvre township of Lamballe.

* * *

Lamballe is a typical Breton township, with whitewashed houses littered along a ridge and the usual large church or churches. All Breton churches seem too large for any possible congregation, a tribute to the religious life of the community.

Lamballe was once the capital of the Counts of Penthièvre, one of the great Breton lordships and it stands above the Gouessant River, one of the minor but attractive streams which flow north to the Channel and across the Val-André.

At this point we veer east, to start our tour along the coast, back to the Côte d'Emeraude, which we reach at little St Jacut, west of Dinard, but you will soon discover that you cannot escape from the sea for long in Brittany.

The Bretons share with the British a national reluctance to see a piece of water without a boat floating on it, and every road seems to lead eventually to the waterside. It is better to accept this as a fact of life and enjoy it, than to struggle, vainly attempting to get away from the sea.

The Côte d'Emeraude is jagged. According to the map it runs from Dinard through St Cast to the wide sandy beaches at Sables-d'Or-Les-Pins. This indented coastline is full of little ports, villages and holiday resorts, perfect for family holidays, and all very much the same. Stay anywhere, take bucket and spade, and hie ye to the plage!

Dominating the Côte, though, is Cap Fréhel. The Cap is, in turn, dominated by a great lighthouse, the one that flashes its welcome and warning way off to the right as you sail in on the dark dawn towards St Malo. Michelin states that the light can be seen 70 miles away when the weather is good, and only 200 yards away when it is bad, which says something about the weather on this part of the coast.

The cape is comprised of colourful cliffs, nearly 300 ft. high, in dull pinks and greys, and on a fine day the contrast between the rose-coloured rocks, and white surf and the blue sea is startling, while below the cliffs, thickly clustered on the rocks, is a host of seabirds. Gulls, terns, cormorants, all swoop and soar over the waves, their cries piercing the dull boom and crash of the waves far below. You can view these cliffs by sea, taking an excursion from Dinard, but from any angle, Cap Fréhel is the dominating feature of the Emerald coast.

Behind you and to the east, across the Anse or Bay-of-Sevignes

41

lies the Vauban fortress of La Latte. This is imposing even at a distance and grows in stature as you approach.

La Latte was built by the pirate family of Goyon-Matignon in the Middle Ages and restored by Vauban in the 17th century. A menhir, or standing stone, called *Gargantua's Finger*, guards the landward approach, but La Latte is truly magnificent viewed from the sea. In France a château can be any large country home, but a fortified castle is a *château-fort*. La Latte has all the attributes of a *château-fort*; the cliffs protect the seaward side, while from the land, a double crevasse spanned by two drawbridges makes another natural defence, before you reach the fortress, which behind contains a double *enceinte,* a cannon-ball factory and barracks for a hundred men-at-arms. Visited in late evening, when the sun is plunging down the western sky behind Fréhel, La Latte is fearsome.

*   *   *

Further along the coast by a series of narrow roads which overlook wide white sandy beaches, each of which will tempt you to stop, you will arrive at the resort of Erquy. Erquy has no less than seven beaches, wide, clean expanses, being uncovered as the tide goes out and proceeding past these beaches will lead you to the Val-André, directly north again of Lamballe.

Protected from the winds by Cap Fréhel on one side and the Tréguier peninsula on the other, Val-André is a mild sheltered region of white beaches backed by pine woods. You can leave the beach for a while and visit the moated château at Bienassis, or the chapel of Notre-du-Bon-Voyage, at St Jacques, but it is the seascapes which make the greatest impact in this part of the Côtes.

West of Val-André lies a vast bay, the Anse d'Yffiniac, stretching between Val André and the Pointe du Roselier, itself inside the even larger Bay of St Brieuc. A minor road leads close to the shore here and the views across the bay, especially at low tide, seem almost endless.

*   *   *

Finally, to end our tour along the Côte d'Emeraude, we arrive at St

Cap Fréhel

Brieuc, which contributes a modern attraction to the traveller — traffic jams!

It is quite easy to circle St Brieuc for some time, unable to penetrate the centre, and find the *Hôtel Beauregard*. This is largely because St Brieuc's roads span two ravines by means of two viaducts. The town centre is dominated by the cathedral of St Stephen, which was begun in the 13th century and burned, sacked, pillaged and generally knocked about until as recently as 1944. However, even here, a typical Breton surprise, you can step back into the past, for unlike many Breton churches, St Stephen's or rather to give it it's French name, St Etienne, is quite small. In the chancel lies the sanctuary of St William, and the cathedral, as you will quicky notice, was once fortified and then severely battered, during the War of the Breton Succession.

Legend has it that the first Bretons to arrive in Armorica, among them St Brieuc, fleeing from the Northmen, landed near what is

43

now St Brieuc in the 5th century A.D. They came ashore near Russe-de-Breha, and must have found the country around St Brieuc, the so-called *Göelo*, quite delightful.

In late Autumn, this country glows with the tall yellow gorse and purple heather, red cider apples blazing on the trees, and the landscape leaps to life as the sun comes out and illuminates the blue sea and the hills behind with a red evening glow. Out of St Brieuc then to view this colourful country, and on for dinner at *La Vieille Tour* at Sans-La-Tour, by the bay and back again to bed as the moon comes up.

3
The Côtes du Nord: The Granit Rose Coast and Trégor

The tide was going out fast. From the terrace of the *Hôtel Columbière* at Etables the rocks of the St Quay reef were surfacing rapidly, while on the widening strand a host of gulls and sea birds were foraging busily in the shallow pools. A pair of field-glasses and a good field-guide is almost essential in Brittany. From the terrace we could spot avocets, curlews, black-backed gulls, cormorants, and a wide variety of terns wading in the shallows or resting on the sand, while the birdsong from the thick brush along the cliffs was almost deafening.

At St Brieuc, which lies a little inland, the coast swings north into the Tréguier peninsula, the 'ears' of the Breton wolf's head, but before heading north for more of these delightful bays and to provide a balance to the Breton scene, you might turn south for a brief visit to the towns of Montcontour and Quintin.

Montcontour is in the Penthièvre district and the central square, the Place de Penthièvre, is a perfect example of early 18th-century architecture. Montcontour stands on a steep hillside and was once completely walled, but apart from the architecture the real reason for coming here is to visit the little chapel of Notre-Dame-du-Haut. You must ask at the farm to the right of the porch for the key, but once inside you will get a delightful surprise.

Breton churches are quite different from those I have found in other parts of France. The Wars of Religion and the Revolution did irreparable damage to the former glories of French religious art and architecture. Churches were sacked, burned and secularized, congregations dispersed, windows smashed, statues defaced or decapitated. Unlike most English parish churches, which are homely affairs, often smelling of flowers and beeswax, the typical French church is today a bare gloomy place, echoing eerily, a pale shadow of some former glory. There are exceptions here and there, but as a rule French churches are depressing, and the visitor can and should be highly selective in those he or she chooses to look at.

Breton churches are different. Quite apart from the architecture, which is in itself rather unique, they are full of interest, colour, and fascinating relics. A travel writer usually has to try hard to prevent his book from being a tour in and out of church doors, and from a host of churches select only his personal favourites, but in Brittany at least, the choice is wide and Notre-Dame-de-Haut is a good example.

Notre-Dame contains six statues to the 'healing' saints. St Mamar cures colic, which is unfortunate since he indicates his power by exposing his entrails. St Léon cures rheumatism, while St Meen is efficacious for nerves. St Hubert will protect you from the bites of mad dogs while St Houarniaule can be invoked against fear! St Eugénie cures headaches, and so, having a hangover, it was before that saint that I lit my particular candle. It worked! But perhaps the aspirin helped a little also.

* * *

Quintin lies to the west, another little town where the church contains the shrine for another pilgrimage, Notre-Dame-de-Delivrance, much prayed to by expectant mothers. The shrine contains a reliquary with a piece of the Virgin's girdle. Quintin stands, or rather overlooks the Gouët River, one of a small network of local rivers all flowing north and east towards St Brieuc, but we go north, past Châtelaudren, to the coast again by the port at Binic. Binic is a fishing port, as your nose will reveal, with a colourful fleet of trawlers, and stands on a wide bay. The coast road runs up to St Quay and then on to Plouha, a significant stop. Here, and if not today then certainly until quite recently, the balance was struck between the French and Breton languages. From now on, as we travel across the old districts of *Göelo, Trégor* and *Finistère*, we are in a region where Breton is the language of the country, of the people, the one they speak at home and among themselves. Breton is now in slow retreat, or perhaps it is more exact to say at low ebb. The tide does appear to be turning, especially among the young who are again actively concerned with their identity as Bretons and their linguistic heritage, and interest in Breton music, language and folk-lore has never been higher.

Plouha is standing up well to the onslaught of tourism, and is a trim, neat little place. Many of the Plouha cottages are owned by old Naval pensioners, who keep their cottages suitably spick and span, and grow very succulent vegetables in their kitchen gardens. Going north, on the left of the Paimpol road, lies the little chapel of Kermaria, in yellow stone, a shady place with a porch full of saints and containing a medieval 'Doom'. A 'Doom' is a vision of the Last Judgement, and they are increasingly rare.

The chapel dates from the 14th century and the Doom here, which takes the form of a Dance of Death, was installed in about 1450. All manner of folk are seen being hurried to Hell, and a scroll on a doleful note reminds us to . . .

> *. . . Leave all your pride*
> *. . . You are not alone*
> *. . . For all of your riches*
> *. . . The richest has only a shroud.*

In some ways the Bretons seem preoccupied with death. Perhaps it is just that as a seafaring people they have seen a lot of it, but it appears as a theme in many of the artistic works. At least they don't seem afraid of it.

*　　*　　*

The coast above Plouha is extremely jagged, broken into a series of peninsulas, the first of which contains Paimpol. Paimpol is a fairly typical Breton town, notable for a pleasant central square and the *Relais Brenner*, on the Pont-Lezardrieux, and it has served as the setting for books by Loti. Press on up the peninsula for the Pointe de l'Arcouest and take the ferry for the little isle of Bréhat, the largest of a score or more which lie off this coast.

Brittany is surrounded by islands, and it would take a lifetime to visit them all, but Bréhat is very pretty and, weather permitting, this is a short and pleasant trip. The rocks here on Bréhat are really red, and the little gardens on the island are crammed with flowers and fig trees.

Beyond Paimpol, to the west, and by taking the bridge over the Trieux estuary, you will arrive at Tréguier. The bridge spans a gorge which the locals hereabouts call a '*ria*', a word more commonly found on the north coasts of Spain, where it means 'estuary'. Further west, in Léon, they call these inlets '*abers*', a word probably derived from the Cornwelsh. The links with Celtic Britain are found everywhere in Brittany.

I like Tréguier and I urge you to visit it, heading immediately on arrival for the church, or rather the cathedral, of St Tudwal (or St Tugwel) who sounds Cornish enough, which is reasonable since according to legend St Tudwal came from Britain and was a relative of King Arthur.

St Tudwal's cathedral contains, and rightly venerates, the tomb of St Yves. His head is kept in a reliquary in the sacristy. St Yves must be one of heaven's busiest saints, for he is the patron saint of lawyers and their clients, and unlike some saints whose life and works are shrouded in antiquity, St Yves definitely existed. He was born near Tréguier in 1253 and studied law in the Schools of Paris. He took Holy Orders in 1285 at Orleans, and then went to serve the Bishop of Rennes, arguing cases in the Ecclesiastical Court, where he rapidly became very unpopular. He wouldn't take bribes; he demanded the truth, and he refused to favour the rich. Well, you can't please everybody. After a stormy career, Yves died in 1303 and was instantly admitted to sainthood. It is interesting that by his tomb lies a plaque placed there by a group of American lawyers, who clearly also found it necessary to come a very long way to seek the intercession of their own particular saint. His feast day is on the 19th May.

St Tudwal's also contains the tomb of Duke John V, who died in 1442. His tomb, and that of St Yves, are recent replacements, the originals having been destroyed in the Revolution and restored quite recently. The church tower, incidentally, is called the Hastings Tower and dates from the 12th century.

Tréguier is an agreeable town in which to spend the day, perhaps visiting the house of Renan, the agnostic writer and philosopher, born here in 1823, or examining the half-timbered houses in the centre, or again, heading downhill to the quay for a drink at the little

Gateway to Tréguier

Café du Port. There are a great many interesting places around Tréguier, apart from the imposing coastline.

The castle at La Roche-Jagu has been recently restored and has splendid views, while to the north lies the quaint little port of Porz-hir. A little way south lies St Yves' birthplace at Minihy-Tréguier. The church there stands on the site of his former home and in the churchyard is a medieval arched monument which pilgrims to St Yves are supposed to crawl under on their knees. I don't think St Yves would approve, although at Jaudy, petitioners to the saint had a much more complicated ritual to undergo, which included throwing a handful of nails through a window, entering the church backwards, and then shouting their request loudly to gain attention!

I like quiet little places and Port Blanc on the coast north of Tréguier is minute, calm, and therefore ideal. When we arrived the tide was out, exposing an encircling reef, and a harbour, or bay, full of jagged rocks. Port Blanc has two good hotels, the *Hôtel des Iles* and the *Grand*. The *des Iles* is, in fact, the grander.

From the dining room at the Grand, while eating lunch, it was interesting to watch the bay change shape and character as the tide came in. The day was calm; there were no waves, and so the remorseless rising of the water was both eerie and beautiful.

"For while the tired waves, vainly breaking
Seem here no painful inch to gain
Far back, through creeks and inlets making
Comes silent, flooding in, the main."

Arthur Hugh Clough's poem springs to the mind by any shoreline in Brittany, and watching the making and ebbing of the tides can become a daily preoccupation, almost mesmeric as the rocks slowly submerge and the beach imperceptibly narrows. You must get used to the action of the tides in Brittany, for they govern the day. The tide flows in, or 'floods' for about six-and-a-half hours, and remains steady, or 'slack water' for a brief period before it 'ebbs' or flows out again. The ebb takes as long as the flood, and there are two tides a day. Each day the time of high tide will be around an hour later than the previous day, and every month there are Spring and Neap tides.

Port Blanc

A Spring tide is one with the highest high tides and the lowest low tides, while a Neap tide has the reverse; lowest high and highest low. Confusing isn't it?

The *Grand* at Port Blanc, just opposite the tiny little chapel of the Virgin atop its rock, is well worth a visit, for the welcome is warm, the Muscadet chilled, the food good and the prices reasonable. If you are very hard to please, they even have Breton specialities such as the *Tom ha ynn*, a crêpe with ice-cream filling, covered with chocolate sauce, and finally flambé'd in Grand Marnier. Very slimming!

The coast road from Port Blanc to Tréburden stays right by the sea, past Perros Guirec and Trégastel-Place, a very picturesque place with its blue-turreted castle on a rock, and our first *Plou* or parish — Ploumanac'h. From Ploumanac'h keen birdwatchers can take a trip to the bird sanctuary on the *Sept Iles*, five miles offshore. You cannot land, but the seabirds are there in their thousands, and include auks and gannets plunging fearlessly into the sea.

Ploumanac'h is attractive, very rocky, with an old customs' patrol path, the *sentier des douaniers*, now serving walkers as an enjoyable trek over to Perros-Guirec. This is a popular seaside resort, with a fine safe beach and an interesting port.

This is a smugglers' coast and further evidence of this lucrative if rather risky activity, can be found at the chapel of Our Lady at La Clarté, built on the highest point hereabouts, to guide ships in to safety in fog or bad weather — and who but smugglers would close this coast in fog?

Beyond La Clarté, up a side road towards the Telecommunications Centre, you will find your first *menhir*, a huge upright stone — the menhir of St Duzec.

Many menhirs, especially the large, solitary and imposing ones, were the site of pagan rites before the Christian era. Too big to be moved, the early missionaries turned these objects into Christian shrines and after due exorcism, carved a cross on to them, although for generations afterwards the local people would still acknowledge the pagan gods as well, just to be on the safe side.

This coast is ideal for the traveller. It is seamed with little valleys, islands, quiet bays and beaches, and even on the most crowded day it is quite possible to find somewhere quiet. When the sun goes down you can always retreat down the coast to Trébeurden or inland to Lannion.

52   *   *   *

Menhir of St Duzec

Locquirec

This part of the coast, between Ploumanac'h and Trébeurden, is often referred to as the Brittany *Corniche* and Trébeurden is particularly famous for its pink rocks, hence the *Granit-Rose*, and for the curious shapes into which they have been eroded. Many of the rocks have acquired curious names, but all should be seen.

Trébeurden overlooks Lannion bay with a selection of islands, giving perfect sailing for small boats in the prevailing westerly winds. The side road through Pleumeur-Bodou, past the domed Space Station, leads you away from the coasts of Brittany *Corniche*, but stay there if you wish, for here as elsewhere there are plenty of byways to explore before you cross the estuary of the Léguer and arrive at Lannion.

Lannion is the southern centre for the *Corniche* and capital of Trégor, and you can turn east again here, along the valley under the escarpment, back towards Tréguier, under the sheltering northern escarpment.

Lannion is a very old town, full of medieval sites. Brélévenez church was built by the Templars and can be viewed after a considerable climb. It has been altered since the Templars' time and if you descend to the crypt and climb to the tower you will ascend from the Romanesque, through the Gothic and arrive, panting, at the Flamboyant. From the tower there are fine views of the town and the river valley.

Lannion is a restful place after the windy wavy coast, and a good centre for excursions. There are plenty of small comfortable hotels and at least one excellent restaurant, the *Auberge de La Porte de France*. They offer all manner of seafood dishes and a wide range of fixed price menus. You will almost certainly have to book ahead, but the wait will be worth the trouble.

The Léguer enters Lannion from the south, and you can follow it down to the ruins of Tonquédec, the chapel at Kerfons, and the castle at Kergrist — *Ker* is a prefix you will encounter frequently in Brittany and it simply means *'place'*. Below Kergrist is the Chapelle les Sept Saints — the Seven Sleepers. It is barely a chapel, more a crypt over which a church has been built.

Wandering south on minor roads, which are always the best roads, you will arrive at Belle-Isle-en-Terre. This is a little place, famous for its wrestlers, wrestling being a popular and ancient Breton sport. When Charles VII was still the Dauphin and glooming around in Bourges waiting for Joan of Arc, wrestlers from Belle-Isle-en-Terre were brought to entertain him.

Nearby are two interesting chapels at Locmaria and Loc-Envel, *loc* being another Breton prefix meaning, as you may guess, a holy place. Both are in the Flamboyant Gothic, very similar to the English Decorated style, and have remarkable wooden screens, but we have many fascinating churches to visit later in Finistère, so you may, if you wish, press on to the Menez-Bré on the road to Guingamp. The Menez-Bré is a hill, almost a thousand feet in height, topped by a chapel. The road up to the summit is very steep indeed, but the views are stupendous. The maps tell you that Brittany is not a mountainous country, and this is factually correct, but it *seems* like one. The countryside is continually rolling and dipping so that these hills which jut up from the mass, like the Menez-Bré, seem much higher than they are.

Guingamp is a weaving centre. One story has it that the word 'gingham' is a corruption of Guingamp and it may be so, although nowadays Guingamp is more notable for food, a reputation which seems to rest on the fine cooking at the *Relais du Roy*. The old town, still with the relics of ramparts, is quite small and contains one of those rare Black Virgins, *'Our Lady of Good Hope'*, in a Gothic basilica. There is a pilgrimage to the Virgin on the first Saturday in July, and only then is Guingamp packed with people.

*   *   *

There are various ways back to the caost, but we go north and west again, across the high land to St Michel-en-Grève, on a wide bay, and so to the little town of Locquirec. So many people told me to visit Locquirec that I was prepared to dislike the place on sight, but it is delightful. There is a small harbour and lots of sandy beaches. The hotels vie with each other in excellence and anyone can choose one at random and be well satisfied.

Locquirec lies west of the Douron river and so, strictly speaking, it lies in the next département of Finistère. It is, for all that, a good centre for another foray south, into the hinterland of the Côtes du Nord, to the castle at Rosanbo which can be visited to see the garden by Le Nôtre. The gorges beyond Loc-Envel are where the streams and rivers run north out of the Argoat. Here, at Lanrivain, near St Nicolas-de-Pélem, you will find your first Breton calvary. This calvary is small but the figures are large and imposing, a foretaste of things to come. So west again, out at last from the comfortable Côtes du Nord, into a region far less familiar, the Breton heartland of Finistère, jutting out into the wild Atlantic, and quite unlike anywhere else.

4

Finistère: The Léonais and Montagnes d'Arrèe

Finistère may be conveniently divided into two regions. This is more convenient that strictly accurate, but it will serve. In the north lies Léon and in the south Cornouaille. In the opening chapter, I described the shape of Brittany as a wolf's head, snapping at the Atlantic. A dog is certainly far too tame. The jaws of this wolf can be imagined as Léon and Cornouaille, while, between them, a panting tongue of land, lies the peninsula of Crozon. This whole region, Finistère, is the Brittany of your imagination, the place of Calvaries and *pardons*, of people in lace coiffes, and a rocky coast beaten by the full fetch of the Atlantic waves.

Our introduction to this region starts, moderately enough, at the little pilgrim town of St Jean-du-Doigt, *St John-of-the-Finger*, above Morlaix, and the name alone should make you want to go there.

St Jean, like many of the villages in Finistère, has a church which seems out of all proportion to the rest of the commune. The reason here is that the church contains a famous relic, a finger of St John the Baptist, brought to the village in 1437, and much venerated ever since. Anne of Brittany came to pray there in 1505 and her gifts helped the local people to complete the great church.

You will have to ask the priest if you wish to see St John's reliquary, one of several in the presbytery, but do take time to stroll around the village and examine the churchyard fountain with its carvings of St John pouring baptismal water from his cup. The architecture is modest and pleasing, the perfect gateway to Finistère.

The coast to the north of St Jean-du-Doigt is another of these

The Baptist Fountain, St Jean du Doigt

Morlaix

typically Breton peninsulas, a maze of rocky coves and sandy beaches, peaceful secret places to make for on a sunny afternoon. To the west lies Morlaix Bay, fed by the estuaries of the Rivers Dossen and Dourduff. Morlaix *ville* itself lies some ten miles inland from the sea and is remarkable on first sight for the huge span of the massive 19th-century granite railway viaduct which towers two hundred feet above the streets of the town. Morlaix lies deep in the valley and was at one time a port. To a certain extent it still is, but nowadays it is mostly yachts and small coastal vessels which find their way even this far inland. The river really divides Finistère from Côtes du Nord, so that one bank is the Quai de Tréguier, while the other is the Quai de Léon.

The recent war and time itself has not dealt too kindly with Morlaix. It has had its share of noble visitors down the years, from Mary, Queen of Scots, and the ubiquitous Duchesse Anne, down to hoards of tourists in our present time, but it remains a small market

59

town and port, mainly interesting as a centre for the country round about and here, in this role, Morlaix shines indeed. You will find comfortable accommodation at the Hotel *Europe* or at the little motel outside the town near the autoroute, and you can eat well along the main street. From Morlaix, those unique treasures of Brittany, the calvaries, are only a few short miles away.

*   *   *

In the mind's eye, the calvaries of Brittany are unique. They are certainly among the sights you go there to see and the memory of them will linger long after you leave, and come home again. They are disturbing and veiled, of course, in religion.

Religion means a great deal in Brittany. Even the atheist or agnostic will be unable to ignore the strong religious presence in Brittany and this does not seem to be the imposed religion of the Church militant. You feel that the people are religious and indeed, many of the pleasant things about Brittany may be rooted in the religious training and background of the people. The typical Breton is hard-working, reasonable, tidy, conscientious, friendly and family-minded. I am also quite certain that, being only human, the Breton matches these virtues with an impressive clutch of vices. Rumour has it that they drink. However, having only visited Brittany as a tourist, the local people have always been nice to me and, since tourists and their hosts do not always see eye to eye, anyone who is able to be consistently pleasant to tourists has my wholehearted support. These attributes are sometimes said to be 'Christian virtues' and, while no religion has a monopoly of decency, in this particular case there may be something in it.

Be that as it may, and it is not a point I would care to labour, you will find the churches of Brittany surprising. If you are a regular traveller in France you will even find them astonishing.

For a start, they are usually large, certainly much too large for their parishes. They are also largely late-Gothic in period and appear to be of even a later date than that. This is largely because they are built of granite, a stone which hardly weathers at all, and so they look much newer than they usually are.

This remarkably good condition is also due to the absence of wholehearted vandalism during the Wars of Religion and the

Parish close, Guimiliau

Revolution, and the signs of care, a tribute to the unrelenting toil of the parishioners. They are, unlike most French churches, full of interesting objects; paintings, carvings, tombs, statues, images and glass, while in one respect at least, they are unique.

* * *

A considerable number of Breton churches, mainly in the West and mostly in Finistère, have that peculiarly Breton addition, the parish close.

A parish close usually consists of three main parts, apart from the Church. There will be a cemetery, a forest of rustic crosses, an *ossuary*, or charnal house, once the gathering place for old bones, and, dominating the scene, an immense and elaborately carved calvary.

61

These calvaries usually consist of carvings depicting the Crucifixion, while, surrounding the crosses will be score, even hundreds, of figures showing scenes from the Old and New Testaments, saints and martyrs, and the odd cautionary tale. These calvaries are remarkable works of art and very often the site of spectacular local pilgrimages or *pardons*.

The calvaries began in the late 16th century during the Counter-Reformation period, or a little later, but they were inspired as much by local rivalry as religious fervour, each village vying with the next to improve and embellish its parish church and the surrounding close.

Morlaix is the ideal centre to see the best of these, so let us now go into the surrounding district and see some of them for ourselves.

* * *

The local Tourist Offices have signposted a circuit of calvaries west of Morlaix, and the first, a bare fifteen miles east of Morlaix, just off the road to Brest, lies at St Thégonnec. This has a large parish close complex, complete with church, calvary, a late 17th-century ossuary, and a triumphal-arch. This complex dates from the late 16th century and the calvary contains scores of figures, notably St Thégonnec and the wolves he trained to pull his plough after they had eaten his horses. There is also a portrayal of Christ at the scourging and Pilate washing his hands. The church porch, with its row of guardian saints, was once the meeting place for the Parish Council, which doubtless spent a good deal of time there wondering how to do down its rival in neighbouring Guimiliau. Guimiliau has another, and possibly more magnificent close, and the calvary, apart from the usual entombment and Crucifixion, also shows the story of that unfortunate damsel, Kate Gollet, who took the devil for her lover and stole holy wafers from the church to please him. You will find her being torn to pieces by demons on one corner of the calvary. The calvaries were often used by the priest for his sermons, each little scene serving to 'point a moral or adorn a tale'.

Lampaul-Guimiliau, a little further on, has yet another close and a tamer calvary, perhaps overshadowed by the magnificent church, but all are in the most wonderful state of preservation. The decoration, and above all the detail, are still intact after almost four

Detail, Calvary at St Thégonnac

hundred years — a tribute to the skill of the craftsmen and the hardness of granite.

You can spend a whole day quite happily visiting these three villages alone, examining the details in the church and close. This indulgence may well satiate your appetite for church architecture, at least for a while, but if you travel on to Landiviseau, you can get a nice family lunch at the *Hotel Floch* before travelling on in the afternoon to see the calvaries at La Roche, La Martique, or Pecran near Landerneau, where again you can eat well at the *Clos du Pontic*, before travelling on for a brief visit to the port and naval base at Brest.

*   *   *

As happened too often in Brittany during the last war, Brest suffered considerably as a result of Allied bombing, French resistance and German tenacity. The port was, and is, a base for the French Atlantic Fleet and was therefore extensively used by German U-Boats, coastal craft and large warships. Their presence led to continual bombing for four years by the Allies, and the town only fell in 1944, after a prolonged siege. Although now rebuilt in an open and agreeable manner, little remains of a historic seaport, which dated back to the Roman times, and present-day Brest need not delay us long on our travels to the West.

On the way out you might care, however, to cast a passing eye at the manor of Keroual, just before Guilers. This was once the home of Louise de Keroual, later Duchess of Portsmouth and mistress of our own Charles II. Louise had a very adventurous career and a host of affairs, even accompanying one lover to the wars while disguised as a cabin boy aboard his warship. She visited England in the train of Charles' aunt, the Duchess of Orleans and, after the minimum of delay, became the King's mistress. Her son by Charles, Charles Lennox, became Duke of Richmond, an English title which usually descended whenever vacant, to some suitable Breton connection.

* * *

West of Brest, and we shall return to the area of Brest itself again later, lies the great snout of Brittany, terminating in the Pointe de St Mathieu, below le Conquet, where we turn north for the fjord-like contours of the *Côte des Abers*.

From anywhere along this coast, look west. The next land out there — almost — is America. The exceptions are the maze of islands off the shore, Molène, Quémenès, Balanec, each with its belt of surf and, on the horizon, the shadowy bulk of Ouessant.

Ouessant, or as the English sailors still call it, Ushant, is still the gateway to Europe for the western voyager. For centuries every sailor made his first landfall at Ushant, to check his position before bearing up for the Channel ports and home, and even today, the lighthouse at de Créac'h beams a welcome to the west.

The island itself is not large, only some ten square miles, but it enjoys a remarkably mild climate, especially in winter, unless, of course there is a gale, in which case the waters around this coast become a maelstorm. If the weather if fair though, there are excursions to the island from Brest and le Conquet, the trip taking about two hours.

Porch, Guimiliau

E

* * *

Ushant is the fly hovering off the nose of the *Léonais*, and back on the mainland and still heading north along the coast you will soon come to the coast of the 'Abers', between Trézien and Brignogan Plage.

Aber, you may think, is a derivative from the welsh *aber*, which means a river mouth, but rivers are the one thing these deep valleys on the north coast do not have. Fjords would be a more descriptive word, for they are steep-sided valleys, probing sharply into the land.

This part of the province is dalled the Côte des Abers, or the *Land of Ac'h*. For centuries it has been the home of the *göemonniers*, people who live by gathering seaweed or sea 'wrack' and piling it on the fields ashore, where, once burnt, it serves as fertilizer.

These smouldering piles of weed can still be seen, although this trade, like so many ancient occupations is no longer what it was, a fact which causes problems for the yachtsmen who frequent this coast. They find that the long seaweed, no longer intensively cropped, is quick to foul their propellers and rudders.

The *Aber* coast is a very beautiful part of Brittany and, like the Cornwall which it so greatly resembles, is a region full of legend.

The castle of Trémazan near Portsall, for example, once sheltered Tristan and Iseult, that tragic couple from the Arthurian legend, and was certainly the birthplace of Tanguy du Chatel, a staunch supporter of the French Crown, who proved the fact in 1419 when he drove an axe into the head of the Duke of Burgundy at Montereau and so removed one of the King's enemies permanently from the scene. The *abers* continue north of Portsall with Aber Benoit, and Aber Vrac'h, both deep valleys in a rocky coast.

Apart from 'abers' or estuaries, we also have *'plou'*, another Breton prefix meaning *parish*. Like the abers, these stand on small peninsulas, each offering peaceful, uncrowded beaches to the visitor.

Pass through the little yachting centre of Aber Wrac'h and you will arrive at Plouguerneau, quite small but with one memorable restaurant, *Las Voyageurs*, and then on to Brignogan, once, like Plouguerneau, the haunt of wreckers.

All through this country you will encounter megaliths, or standing stones. There are supposed to be more here than in any other part of France, mostly in the form of dolmens, that is with two or three stone uprights crowned with a flat boulder, many formerly being burial chambers, and covered with earth. They are not so plentiful as the upright menhirs at Carnac, although there is one great menhir, the '*Men-Marz*', now christianized. They can be seen everywhere and are one of the sights of the region.

Le Folgoët, in the very centre of the Léonais, is a surprise. Having seen the churches at St Thégonnec and Guimiliau, I suppose we should be getting accustomed to fine churches, but those of the parish closes are rather cramped. Le Folgoët, on the other hand, is spread out across a wide village green, and you can stretch your arms wide there and breathe deeply, taking in the scene, peaceful as any village green can be.

Le Folgoët became a pilgrim centre because in the 14th century a simple-minded shepherd lad, called Solomon, lived there. He could speak only a few words, endlessly repeating *"Oh Lady Virgin Mary"*, like a mantra. After his death in 1358, a white lily sprang from his grave, which on being investigated, was found to come from Solomon's mouth, evidence of sainthood and the birth of the legend.

After the Battle of Auray in 1364, the victor, Jean de Montfort, laid the first stones of the church which is now the pilgrim centre of Notre-Dame-de-Folgoët. The church was completed in 1423 and is another place which no visitor to Brittany should miss. It was built in the most exquisite style of the late Gothic, in hard-wearing Kersanton blue granite, and the architecture, both inside and out is quite magnificent.

Le Folgoët was famous enough to attract the Duchesse Anne in 1505 and the mob in 1793, but the local stone stood up well to their rustic battering, and most of the statuary and bracing still survives. The interior of the church is striking and the hall opposite, with the cardinals' arms in the porch (now a museum) is a Renaissance jewel.

Le Folgoët lies in the centre of the Léonais and you can return towards Morlaix through Kerjean and Lambader for further forays.

The castle at Kerjean now belongs to the State and very stately it is. It has been referred to as the 'Versailles of Brittany', but that, on size alone, is greatly overstating the case, while in no way diminishing Kerjean's other attractions.

It stands at the end of a long tree-lined drive and is protected by a moat. Moats were a trifle unnecessary for the period in which

Church of Our Lady, Le Folgoët

Kerjean was built, between 1560 and 1590, but Brittany is the place for moated castles, which is no doubt why the builder, Louis Barbier, provided one.

It is a Renaissance manor, built on a central square. The entrance is across a drawbridge and through an arch, where on one side you will see the pigeon-loft and on the other the pillars of the gallows from which the Lord of Kerjean exercised his role as magistrate and hanged the local malefactors. A few guards and a hangman were very necessary residents in the hall of the 16th-century French noble, although, such are the twists of history, the last owners of Kerjean were themselves guillotined in 1794.

Berven, to the north, has another calvary, but of no great merit, and you can press on past Lambader, which has another late-Gothic church, and so back to Morlaix.

* * *

Morlaix is a market centre for the Northern Léonais, but hardly the place to stay. Hotels in Brittany, especially on the coast, are plentiful but in fact Morlaix has very few hotels and only one, the *Europe* is of any merit.

To the north though, staying close to the 'ria', or estuary of the Penze, you can reach two interesting towns, firstly St Pol-de-Léon with its remarkable church, and secondly the Channel ferry port of Roscoff.

St Pol was the seat of the first bishopric in Brittany and takes its name from St Paul — or St Pol, the Aurelian, but a cathedral only remains a cathedral while it contains the seat of a bishop, and the Bishopric of St Pol has long since disappeared.

The church of St Pol, which is not large but very well-proportioned, is now overshadowed by the nearby 14th-century chapel of the Krisker, where the belfry, itself inspired by the Norman spires at Caen, was in turn the model for all those towers and pinnacles we have seen and will see in Brittany; but I fear to weary you of churches in this chapter, so on now to Roscoff, which I admit has a church. However, it also has an interesting aquarium, medieval walls, some nice houses and gardens in the old *bourg* and a fine port which ships out all the local produce and, most notably, the artichoke, the 'almost-emblem' of Breton agriculture. Personally, I think the artichoke a considerably over-rated vegetable. The whole region around St Pol and Roscoff is a market garden area, so *all* the vegetables are superb.

Roscoff was, and to an extent still is, the departure point for the Breton onion sellers who were once a regular sight on the roads of England, pedalling along on their onion-festooned bicycles, and appearing at the back door for a chat and a rapid sale.

Off Roscoff, a mere ten minutes by boat, lies the little isle of Batz, while from the town itself you can look south across the bay to the spires of St Pol, and the little town of Carentec, another seaside resort of considerable charm, on yet another peninsula.

* * *

The sea dominates Brittany. Wherever you go, there it is. Since the Breton shores are attractive, this is no great hardship, but a voyage, like a book, must have variety, so let us now go inland, away from the sea, as far as that is possible in Brittany, to the Argoat and the Montagnes Arrée.

Château, Kerjean

Breton woods and walks

Armorica you will recall, means *'the land facing the sea'*. The Argoat, on the other hand, means *'the country of wood'*, and refers to the hinterland of the region. Once upon a time this might have been very true, but today much of the great Breton forest land has gone. That said, Brittany is still a very woody country, and if there are few great forests there is no lack of woodland, and great oak trees.

South of Morlaix lies Huelgoat, capital of the Argoat, and to the east the Montagnes d'Arrée and the gateway to the *Parc Regional d'Armorique*. A glance at a topographic map will show you just how rumpled this country is, and although the 'mountains' are not high, and technically anyway, not mountains at all, they are rolling and rugged enough. The *Parc Regional d'Armorique* covers most of the

71

Montagnes d'Arrée, and begins in the west at le Faou, running east and a little north towards Huelgoat. Trévezel Rock, north-west of Huelgoat, at 384 metres (1248 ft.) is the ideal place from which to view the mountains to the south and the sea-coast to the rear.

Huelgoat is the centre of great walking country. From the River Argent in the middle of the town, marked walks and *Randonnée* trails lead off in all directions, along steep paths. Although not really high with all the hills hereabouts being less than 700 ft. it certainly seems hilly. Not far from the centre lies the *'roche tremblante*, the rocking stone, which, although weighing over two tons will sway if you put your shoulder to it.

All the *sentiers* have names, and it would take a week to walk them all. The woods are beautiful in autumn, full of rushing brooks with little waterfalls, and the town is full of good hotels, very popular all the year round with hikers and fishermen. One good excursion would be to walk through the woods for lunch at the little routier café, the *Amis des Routiers* on the road south to Carhaix.

The main mass of the Montagnes d'Arrée lies to the west of Huelgoat and a series of little roads will lead you into it. Always take the most minor roads for they alone will take you to those out-of-the-way places.

The Arrée countryside is very varied with its open moors and forests, and the St Michel reservoir provides a huge lake in the centre near Brasparts where, inevitably, the local people keep their boats.

Brasparts itself lies below the height of St Michel de Brasparts. There is a chapel on the top of this mount, or *menez*, from which you can see far across the countryside, north-west to the peninsula of Plougastel-Daoulas, famous for strawberries and the shipping in the Brest roads. Directly west lies another height of *Ren-ar-Hoat-ar-Gosse*, very Breton, and you skirt this on the D42 before running down to le Faou.

Michelin tells us that the little town of le Faou is remarkably pretty when the tide is in. With my usual unerring accuracy I managed to arrive at full ebb, when le Faou stands alone in a wilderness of mudflats and marshes. On the other hand, there was the eventual advantage of watching the tide come in and actually seeing le Faou turn into the pretty place of reputation.

Le Faou stands at the very tip of the Brest roads, that vast and perfect anchorage which leads through the Goulet channel out to the Atlantic, and was once itself a medieval port.

The road will take you a little way north to Daoulas and on to another great calvary at Plougastel-Daoulus (where Kate Gollet again appears with her tormentors) from where you can go for a little tour of that peninsula, or *presqu'ile* or "almost-an-island", before returning to le Faou and preparing for our next stage south into the land of Cornouaille.

5

Southern Finistère: Cornouaille to Quimperlé

The Ménez-Hom, at the head of the Presqu'ile de Crozon is a windy moorland hill, a thousand feet above the sea, dominating the neck of the peninsula, and a little way south of le Faou.

To reach it from le Faou you run along the estuary past some moored warships of the Reserve Fleet, swinging on their rusty anchor chains, and over the Aulne bridge at Térenez. Notice the Aulne, for it is an interesting river and not only here at the beautiful wooded estuary but also further inland around Châteaulin. The sparkling Aulne has salmon and sea-trout, and you could walk across it dry-shod on the decks of a thousand craft. Once across, and past the calvary at Argol, you have a choice and can take both in turn, but first drive on into Ste-Marie-du-Ménez-Hom, park by the church and walk across the moor and bracken up to the Ménez-Hom itself. From the crest you get immense views in every direction, but your gaze will be directed naturally to the west, over the Presqu'ile.

The huge bay you see to the south is the Bay of Douarnenez and, at the neck of the Cap de La Chèvre which juts south, lies the resort of Morgat. Morgat is, not surprisingly, a sailing centre, wonderfully sheltered within the great bay and with excellent walks across the crest of the peninsula to the rival resort of Camaret on the Toulinquet reach. Camaret, which is more exposed to rough seas than Morgat, does have several off-setting advantages. I am not myself a great lover of shellfish, but those who are should make directly for Camaret, the premier lobster port of France. There are a number of

74

good restaurants around the *quai*, usually full of Frenchmen eating at the tops of their voices.

Those of a more intellectual turn of mind will be interested in the pilgrim chapel of Rocamadour, or in visiting the Naval Museum. It was off Camaret, in 1801, that the American inventor, Robert Fulton, put his prototype submarine to its first test. His craft was small and leaky and could only just submerge, but a British frigate, blockading Brest came conveniently into the bay and Fulton and his crew duly gurgled below and set off to sink her. Fulton's submersible was propelled by oars and after floundering around below the surface of the bay for some hours, they surfaced, gasping, to discover that the frigate had hauled her sheets and sailed away. However, Fulton's shade should, and perhaps does, reflect that the German U-boat fleet sailed from this coast during the Second World War and wrought more destruction on the British than the early pioneer could ever have imagined.

The Crozon peninsula is divided at the tip into three smaller outcrops, of Roscanvel, Penhir and Cap de la Chèvre. At the risk of repeating a previous point, can I assure you that each contains little bays, quite deserted in the busiest months, and this region is well worth exploring.

*　*　*

The Bay of Douarnenez can be reached along the coast, or by Châteaulin on the Aulne, a great fishing centre. This would be my chosen route, for after lunch on local trout or salmon at the *Auberge Ducs de Lin* you can press on to Pleyben.

Permit me to rave about Pleyben. The church and calvary at Pleyben are quite outstanding and the setting for both, amid tall trees, is quite magnificent. The church is part-Gothic and part-late-16th-century, all blending wonderfully well, while the figures in the calvary are extremely delicate, and although carved in the late 16th century, they are dressed in the mid-15th-century style and seem for that reason more believable. The interior of the church is the light and airy style of the early Baroque, with fine statues and a blue star-spangled barrel vault.

After Pleyben — and you may have to drag yourself away — it is on up the Valley of the Aulne to Châteauneuf du Faou, where the

75

Playben

river is really beautiful, before returning to Pleyben. Locronon, a little to the south, is unremarkable except once in every seven years when, on the second Sunday in July, begins a week-long religious festival, but you have missed it until 1986, although a smaller one-day affair is held every year.

From here it is back towards the coast and Douarnenez, where you can enjoy another excellent meal and look out on the pleasing vista of the seaport from the *Restaurant Les Mouettes*, on the Plage du Ris. Try the *'jambon au Madère'* with a bottle of chilled Muscadet.

Douarnenez is a holiday centre, but first and foremost it is a commercial fishing port. You will need to skirt the commercial port before you arrive at the *quai*, where the fishing boats are tied up in rows. Painted in all colours, reds, greens, ambers and yellows, they glow on the water in the evening sun. Further on towards Audierne, you will pass beside a creek where the hulls and hulks of old boats are rotting away in the mud, for here, as elsewhere, the fishing is not what it was.

*   *   *

A minor road outside Douarnenez will take you west, along the north shore of the Sizun peninsula. This is by far the best way to reach the Pointe du Raz, being less *touristique* and half way along on the right, lies the nature reserve of Cap Sizun. Seabirds are a feature of Brittany and are nowhere seen to better advantage than at Sizun. You will need good fieldglasses and a head for heights, and bird-watchers will only be admitted to the Reserve in small parties, but the birds can be seen in great numbers and variety. Gulls galore of course, but also auks, kittiwakes, cormorants, puffins on the grassy slopes, as well as ravens and choughs on the steep cliffs along the shore.

This northern route is much less developed than the southern one and brings you out on the Pointe du Van, overlooking the beautiful, but sinister, *Baie des Trépassés*, the 'Bay of the Dead'. Onshore currents bring the bodies of drowned sailors in here, from craft wrecked on the reefs of the Pointe du Raz, a discovery which made the blue waters seem suddenly uninviting.

Under the waters of the Bay of the Dead lies the legendary city of Y's. Whether Y's ever existed is debatable. It is as legendary as Lyonesse but, so the legend goes, it was the capital of Cornouaille, and the home of a King Gradlon whose daughter, Duhat, fell in love with the Devil. The Devil asked her to open the sluices which kept the seas from the town and as the waters drowned the city, he deserted her. She fled for safety with her father, but the waves were overtaking them when a heavenly voice directed the king to cast his daughter into the waves. The king obeyed, losing his daughter and his city to the seas off Trépassés.

We will meet King Gradlon again at Quimper, where he retreated after the flood. The bay, then, is not just a beautiful place, but like so

Baie des Tréspassés

many other places in Brittany, a place of legend and superstition, where the sea beats in from the west and cares very little for anyone who gets in the way. For all that, the bay is very attractive, and you sweep down and up to the lighthouse and cliffs of the Pointe du Raz, looking out over the Raz de Sein and the Ile de Sein itself.

This is a dangerous, villianous coast, frightening in a westerly gale, when the waters become a maelstrom of huge waves and hurtling spray. People come out here to view the storms in winter as well as the blue seas in summer, and their constant feet have worn all the grass off the Pointe, exposing the bare rock and making this a bleak, if beautiful, place.

The Ile de Sein, which can be visited from Audierne is an interesting place, mainly because of the inhabitants. They may appear no different from other Breton people, but they have unusual qualities. The men are fishermen, and all the work ashore, even in the small fields and gardens, is women's work. The men won't touch it. In former times the men made a better living by wrecking, luring ships

79

The Pointe du Raz

on to the rocks where they could be pillaged, another activity shared, once upon a time, by their kinfolk in Cornwall. Do you remember the old prayer?

Lord, we pray there may be no wrecks
But if there be, then let them fall
Upon the coast of Cornwall
For the benefit of the poor inhabitants

Well, as they say, it's all ill wind . . .

However, in the last war, the men of the Sein showed sterner qualities. After a public meeting, the *entire* male population of the island sailed for England in June 1940, and enlisted with the Free French. This included a thirteen year old boy who was most annoyed at being packed off to school immediately on arrival. General de Gaulle remarked at his first review, how strange it was that "*little Sein had provided me with a quarter of the soldiers of France.*"

80

Once home again, and proudly displaying their Medal of the Liberation which de Gaulle awarded to the island, the men soon discovered a new industry. From the days of the Ancien Regime, the inhabitants of Sein have been exempt from such taxation as the *gabelle*, or salt tax. When income tax was universally introduced in France, they were excluded from this also, since the revenue from such a bleak and barren spot would hardly be worth collecting. However, in 1949 the French Government were somewhat put out to discover that the islanders were offering their home to industry as a tax haven! An Act was rushed through, introducing taxation there, to scotch this idea, at which the islanders promptly went on a tax strike. The end of it all was to effectively discourage big business while leaving the islanders still enjoying their immemorial rights.

Audierne, on the south shore of Cap Sizun, is another fishing port, and a great centre for *langoustines*, best eaten locally at the little restaurant *Le Goyen*, (named after the local river) in the Place Jean-Simon, where, apart from the delicious seafood, the food is well served with vegetables grown on the local hills, for Audierne, like Roscoff, is a market centre. St. Tugen, nearby, built after 1500, is a place of pilgrimage, where the saint is said to provide an effective safeguard against rabies. His 'pardon' on the 24th June is always well supported for this reason.

From Audierne we move south, across another immense bay, the Bay of Audierne, to the lonely calvary at Tronoën, and the Pointe de Penmarch. Unlike most calvaries which stand in villages, that at Tronoën is out in the country. As this is the oldest calvary in Brittany, perhaps this one follows the original intention, to build them in lonely places, away from the haunts of men. After all, the first one was '*without a city wall*' and this one at Tronoën is certainly the most moving of them all, and considering its age is in remarkably good condition.

The rocks at Guénolé are another trap for ships, but the Museum of Prehistory there is worth visiting before you press on into Morbihan, the most famous region of Brittany for menhirs and megaliths.

* * *

From here, at Penmarch, we turn north, to Pont l'Abbé and enter the so-called 'Bigouden' district, home of the most familiar of all the

Pont l'Abbé

Breton *coiffes*, a tall white pillar worn high on the top of the head. How it stays in place in all winds and weathers is a mystery to me, but the ladies (and alas, only old ladies, seem to wear it now) manage very well. I saw one lady, head erect, indifferent to the winds of the Pointe de Raz, while we were met at Pont l'Abbé by a lady in a tall *coiffe* pedalling madly downhill on a bicycle, again without loss of her crowning glory.

Pont l'Abbé is the centre of the *pays bigouden*, the part of Brittany which has best retained its old traditions, and is worth a visit for the certainty of seeing one of the Breton *coiffes*. It is also a good centre for exploring the Bigouden country itself, up to the capital of Cornouaille at Quimper.

To the east now, for we are on the southern coast of Brittany. You proceed across the new toll bridge over the Odet into Benodet, which to be positive again, I can recommend as *the* place to stay when visiting the Bigouden coast. It has fine clear waters with good sailing and is very popular with the British, and yachtsmen of all nations. It also has a delightful wooded hinterland, and offshore lie the Glénan islands, home of a famous sailing school and a great sanctuary for seabirds, which can be visited from Benodet or Concarneau.

Quimper, on the River Odet, is very clearly a capital city, although quite small with only 60,000 people, and dominated by the huge Gothic façade of St Corentin's cathedral. This was built between the 12th and 15th centuries and so was entirely completed within the Gothic period. Well, almost completely. The two spires which top the towers were only added in the last century, but they are extremely fine, and blend in exactly with the original building. The mounted figure between the two towers is King Gradlon, King of the City of Y's.

Gradlon retired to Quimper after his kingdom disappeared and was consoled by St Corentin. Until the Revolution, the townsfolk would send the King a drink, once a year, on St Cecilia's Day. The man who climbed the tower would offer the drink to the King — which was naturally refused— down it himself, then throw the glass into the crowd below. Anyone catching it unbroken, which must have been a fairly hazardous task, earned a handsome prize provided by the Town Council, who would go to considerable lengths, like filing through the glass stem, to see that unbroken catches were very rare events.

Benodet

Opposite the cathedral lies the old town, well worth wandering through, especially along the Rue Kéréon, with its old houses and fine shops. There is a range of good restaurants along the Avenue de la Gare, and a comfortable night available at the *Hôtel La Tour d'Auvergne*, named after the Breton soldier who fought with surpassing gallantry in the Napoleonic wars. The hotel is decorated with frescoes depicting his exploits and the one outside the dining room is particularly apt, showing the gallant grenadier storming a Prussian camp crying *"Qui veut diner, me suit!"* "Those who want to dine follow me!" He clearly knew how to inspire French soldiers to the charge.

The Brittany Museum near the cathedral is a must for visitors to Quimper. It offers a complete record of Breton history, and, most unusually in a museum, offers folklore as well as factually correct historical exhibits. So much of Brittany's history is based on legends that any account which leaves them out, while possibly more accurate, remains sterile. On the opposite side of the cathedral is the Musée des Beaux Arts, which has a fine collection of paintings,

84

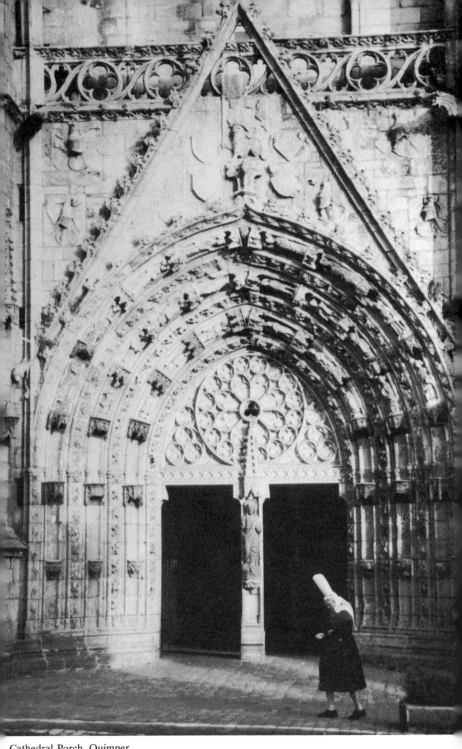

Cathedral Porch, Quimper

including some by Fragonard and Corot, and this will make a useful introduction to the artistic milieu we will shortly visit at Pont-Aven. For a tour of the Odet estuary you can take a boat from Quimper down to Benodet itself.

For Pont-Aven go south to Fouesnant, where the *Hotel Armorique* has an unsurpassed table and across the bay a fine view of our next major stop, the fishing port and walled town of Concarneau.

Concarneau is a fishing port. Yes, another one. This, as you may discover, is the snag with Brittany. It lives from the sea and, on the face of it, when you have said *that* you have said, if not everything, then a very great deal. On the other hand, their ports are all different and Concarneau is one of the most unusual.

It began and developed on the island in the centre of the harbour, now occupied by the *ville close*. A walk around the walls of the *'ville close'* with the colourful moored fishing fleet all about you is the highlight of your visit, and if you can manage to arrive on the third Sunday in August, you can see the port at its best during the *Bleu Filet* fête, when the blue nets of the port's fishermen are hung everywhere among a host of bunting and the gay costumes of the fisherfolk.

Concarneau, naturally enough is full of good restaurants and the food is especially good at *La Belle Etoile*, on the Cabellou-Plage.

*   *   *

East of Concarneau lies Pont-Aven — not in itself remarkable, although an agreeable resort, but centre once for Paul Gauguin and his friends who developed the style which has since become famous as the Pont-Aven school.

Gauguin moved to Pont-Aven from Paris in 1886, and soon began to attract a group of followers. By 1888, after a short visit to Panama by Gauguin, this group had become a self-supporting community, and Gauguin began, with another painter, Emile Bernard, to develop a unique style of painting, peculiarly his own, going far beyond the Impressionist style. The established painters painted what was *there*, the Impressionists painted what they *saw*, which is by no means the same thing, while Gauguin believed in painting what he *felt*.

There is the one story of Gauguin finding one of his friends, Serusièr, painting in the woods near Pont-Aven. *"How do you see that tree?"* he asked him. *"You say yellow, very well. That shadow is blue — let it be pure ultramarine, and as for these red leaves, they seem to me to be vermilion."* Gauguin and Bernard called this style *Cloisonnism* (partitioning), and the effects were, as you can imagine, quite startling. In Gauguin's case, the violent colour contrasts were enhanced by jagged shapes, sharp outlines and flat layers of colour, a complete departure from the Impressionist ideal.

In 1890 Gauguin and Bernard exhibited their work, which had been barred from the official display, in a café next to the central hall of the Paris Exhibition. Their exhibition presented a hundred paintings, and none were sold, but certain critics did at least begin to grasp what the Pont-Aven school was trying to say, "that in art it is more creative to interpret than to copy".

Pont-Aven today still attracts artists. The River Aven, which pours through the town, no longer drives the mills it powered a hundred years ago, but much of the town remains as it was in Gauguin's day. The *Moulin de Rosmadec* still stands, and the food is excellent, while in the centre, the *Hôtel d'Ajoncs*, recalls another of Gauguin's friends, Theodore Botrel, a poet, who lived in Pont-Aven, and started an arts festival, the *Fête des Fleurs d'Ajoncs*, the 'gorse flower festival', still held here in early August. From the centre you can walk up the valley, through the Bois d'Amour to the chapel at Tremelo, where Gauguin painted his "yellow Christ," and back along the river bank, a walk made a thousand times by the paint-spattered artists of the Pont-Aven school.

*   *   *

If you go east again, you will cross several estuaries, for this south coast has more large rivers than that of the north, until you come to the banks of the Laîta, where you turn north for Quimperlé. This road will take you into the forest of Carnoët, pleasant enough now, but one with a grisly tale to tell, another of those Breton legends we mentioned earlier, quite unlikely and yet frequently believed.

Here, long ago, lived the Count of Carnoët, who heard from a fortune-teller that his first-born son would kill him and inherit his lands. He therefore murdered his wives as soon as they became pregnant! His fifth wife managed to flee before the news broke, and eventually bore a son, who became St Trémeur.

Eventually the Count met the saint and, recognising him instantly

The Knight of St Columb, Quimperlé

as his son, (this is a *legend*, you will appreciate) chopped off his head! The saint, quite undaunted, picked up his head and followed the Count back to his castle. There he threw a handful of earth against the walls, at which the entire place collapsed on top of the wicked baron. Exactly *how* St Trémeur became a saint we never discover, but he is shown in statue carrying his head around, and this, apparently, saints were able to do at will. Brittany is supposed to have over 7000 saints, so naturally it must have been difficult to be different.

There is also the story of a priest who told a very sceptical lady the story of St Denis who, although beheaded in Montmartre, was able to carry his head ten miles to his church of St Denis outside the city. *"Ten miles, madame"* said the priest. *"Now* that *was a miracle."* *"One step would have been a miracle"* replied the lady. But the point of a legend isn't that it's true, but that it's believed!

Quimperlé, on the very border of Finistère, hard against Morbihan, is in the valley of the Lafta, a river formed by the joining of two smaller streams, the Isole and the Elle, which join at Quimperle. The town centre is over-shadowed by a massive church, St. Michael, and filled by the bulk of another church, St Croix.

St Croix was first built in the early 12th century in the style of the Holy Sepulchre in Jerusalem, probably from drawings brought home by the victorious survivors of the First Crusade. Solid as it now appears, the church collapsed in the last century, and had to be rebuilt, luckily in the same style, although the rebuilt belfry, cause of the original collapse, now stands apart from the main church.

Quimperlé was some nice old houses, notably in the Rue Dom-Morice, a very short street, where, I had heard, the houses leaned so far towards each other that the inhabitants could shake hands from the upstairs windows. All lies of course, unless they had very long arms, but an attractive street for all that.

When you emerge into the Rue Bremond d'Ars, cross the road and go into the garden of the now ruined church of St Colomban. On the wall is the effigy of a 12th-century knight, still in excellent condition with broad sword and touches of the original paint and gilding, and for all the other charms of this attractive town this little garden is my favourite spot in Quimperlé.

* * *

So, for a while anyway, it is goodbye to Finistère, the most unusual and "un-French" of all the Breton départements. As you will have gathered, you could spend a lifetime exploring the thousand little valleys and coves and hidden places, and any time you have to spare could not be better spent, but it is time to go north again, to le Faouët, and the land of *Mor-bi-han*, the land of the little sea.

6
The Western Morbihan: Le Faouët to Lorient

The northern road from Quimperlé runs quickly into woods. I drove up here in the autumn sunlight and by the Roche au Diable, the wind was blowing the yellow leaves off the trees in a golden snow storm, covering the roads in a thick colourful carpet.

The Roche au Diable is a chaos off the road to le Faouët and overlooks the River Isole, a jumble of huge rocks and narrow footpaths. The view from the rocks, down to the river is obscured by the trees, so a brief stop then to stretch the legs before pressing on past St Fiacre to le Faouët.

Le Faouët is the centre for visiting the Montagnes Noires, a range of wooded hills running across the centre of Finistère. They are fairly well forested and, like most Breton mountains, not particularly high, and in reality not mountains at all but good walking country for all that. Le Faouët itself is a pleasant place, remarkable only for a huge market hall, dating from the mid-1500s. If you go inside, the network of beams and rafters is fantastic.

East of le Faouët, past the chapel of St Nicolas, lies Kernascléden. There is a wide choice of little chapels in this area, and all are worth visiting, especially on foot along the *sentiers*, but to be selective, choose the one at Kernascléden, acclaimed as a masterpiece of the Breton Gothic. It was built in 1453, the year the English were finally expelled from France, and is built with rare skill and attention to detail. Breton churchs tend to feature six apostles in the porch, but Kernascléden has two porches and manages, therefore, to fit in all twelve. The interior is a riot of stone and fresco, and there is another

91

'*Doom*' which illustrates in gruesome detail the tortures which await the Damned after they arrive in Hell.

From Kernascléden you can proceed by minor road north and east to Pontivy on the River Blavet.

If you study a topographic map, which is always a useful thing to have, you will notice that the Blavet runs down a valley from the Forest of Quénécan, out to the sea at Lorient and skirting the hills of the Landes de Lanvaux.

From Pontivy, where you can stay comfortably at the *Hôtel Porhoet*, you can tour north to the little village of Mur-de-Bretagne and around the great lake at Guerlédan.

The Canal de Nantes-Brest runs through here, deserted now, but the towpath is intact and provides a good walking route through the *Argoat*. Some parts of this area are carved into deep rocky gorges like those of Poulancre nearby, and these have quite different scenery from the farming countryside round about, which is largely devoted to mixed agriculture, forestry and quarries.

Pontivy has an old '*bourg*' with the remains of a moated medieval châteaufort, and a new town, built during the First Empire and known for a while as Napoléonville, partly to note the town's loyalty to the Emperor, partly to celebrate the opening of the canal, which was constructed on the Emperor's orders to divert his coastal shipping away from the Royal Navy.

Market Hall, le Faouët

Pontivy is the chief market town of central Brittany and, if you turn south here, you can run down the Blavet, a winding, little-known river, and take in a number of interesting spots on the way.

The Blavet has been much exploited by minor industry, such as saw-mills, but of the local sort, without any satanic smoke-stacks, and the river water is still pure enough for good fishing and therefore well fringed with *pêcheurs*.

St Nicodème and St Nicolas-des-Eaux are two little villages on the river, both with interesting chapels. You can get a good view of the river before you come down to Baud and visit the Venus of Quinipily.

Baud itself is minute and can be quickly visited, and is best seen on market days or Sundays when the older ladies wear their coiffes. You can then go out on the N24 and turn off to see the Venus on her little hill.

She stands in a farmyard, overlooking the empty basin of a large, bath-tub-like fountain. The stone statue is more than life-size, and rather resembles the lid of a mummy's tomb, so that the Eastern and pagan origins are immediately obvious.

The origins of the figure are unknown, but she has an Egyptian aspect, is certainly over 2,000 years old, and far from beautiful. One theory maintains that she was brought from Egypt by one of the occupying legions in about 46 B.C., and she was certainly in Brittany when the first Christian missionaries arrived in about AD 250 for they took violent exception to such a pagan image and the Venus was promptly hurled into a nearby river. This happened frequently down the centuries without avail, for she was always secretly retrieved and replaced by the local people. The priests then hurled her back into the river and again she would be recovered. She was eventually hidden in a cave and remained there until she was placed over the fountain in 1695 and, somewhat worn out by all this excitement, had to be taken down, recarved in the late 1700s, and restored to her present position where she stands, come wind, come weather, greeting the visitor with an enigmatic and rather weary gaze, which, after all she had been through, is hardly surprising.

*   *   *

Hennebont is a surprise. It starts as a straggling village, a typical *village-rue*, and you may be just about to give up and go elsewhere when you reach the main square, the Place Maréchal-Foch, and are at once delighted. Hennebont must join that list of places in Brittany which every traveller should see. It also contains the *Château de Locguénolé*, a fine hotel and restaurant on the banks of the river, where the food is excellent. Opposite the cathedral is the *Hôtel de la Poste* which is much cheaper, serves good food and attracts crowds of local people for lunch on Sunday.

The Place Foch is dominated by the great church of Our Lady of Paradise, which really is huge and, in that small town, quite overwhelming.

The traveller in Brittany will be struck by the number of churches dedicated to Our Lady. Most of the Breton churches were built in the 12th and 13th centuries when the idea of chivalry was taking root in Western Christendom, and, among other things, this meant a rise in the status of women. Previously, women had been little more than chattels, useful for their dowry and to breed sons. Chivalry became symbolized by the ideas of courtly love and this led to the cult of the Virgin. Previously, churches had been dedicated to a local saint and were frequently erected on a former pagan site, consecrated by the early Church. Most of the Breton churches we see today though, are survivals from the Late Gothic and often built in the Flamboyant or Decorated style. Romanesque churches were very rare, having been destroyed by the Northmen, and as most churches in Brittany were built in enduring granite, churches from a later period were largely superfluous. Indeed Breton churches are almost always too large for any possible congregation.

Our Lady of Paradise was built well after the town itself, in the years between 1513 and 1530. The town itself is, or was, of much earlier date and was walled in 1237.

The last war destroyed much of old Hennebont and only remnants of the old walls remain, but you can climb up on them and walk down to the Blavet, looking down into the gardens, and the streets of the town.

The river is still capable of taking coastal craft and the town was once a port. In 1345 an English fleet sailed up the river to lift the siege of the town, then under attack by the French. The English held Hennebont for twenty-seven years before it fell eventually and inevitably to Duguesclin.

* * *

Medieval gateway, Hennebont

Hennebont was once a port, but Lorient on the Blavet estuary still is, and, since the 17th century Lorient has been one of the great Naval arsenals of France. It suffered considerably in the last war so for a better view, and to start your visit, travel down the left bank of the river to the Vauban fortress of Port Louis.

The French too had an East India Company, and so indeed did the Dutch. The *Compagnie des Indes* was financed by the King and private speculators. Louis XIII and Richelieu originally established the company at Port Louis, but Colbert later moved it to Le Havre, where the English took such a toll of the ladened Indiamen as they made their way home up the Channel that Louis XIV and his Chief Minister, Mazerin, re-established the company at the specially built port of Lorient, or L'Orient, and the *'des Indes'* became the more resonant-sounding *Compagnie de L'Orient*.

The port of Lorient, which lies inside the estuary, was protected by the fortress town of Port Louis on the point. This was also built by

95

Lorient and submarine pens

Richelieu, and named after Louis XIII, although it was originally called Blavet. Port Louis today is a tribute to the military genius of Vauban and the perfect example of 17th-century military fortification. The citadel of the port, which is reached across a sea-moat by a narrow drawbridge, now contains a Naval museum. The neighbouring fosse contains a memorial to Resistance fighters shot for spying on the movements of U-Boats operating from the German submarine pens you can see across the estuary in Lorient.

The German submarine fleet ravaged British shipping in the Atlantic from the first days of the war, when a U-boat sank the liner *Athenia* with great loss of life. The submarine menace really expanded with the fall of France in June 1940, when the German Navy obtained possession of the Breton ports of Brest, Lorient and St Nazaire, and gained much extra range. Any details of submarine activity were vital to Allied Naval Intelligence and the local French Resistance took great risks to obtain them, frequently, as we see here, with fatal results to themselves. Allied air raids on the submarine bases led to the construction of bomb-proof submarine pens, some of which you can still see from the walls of Port Louis. The pens were persistently bombed, which did more damage to the surrounding townships than to the U-boats within, and, in the course of the raids, the centres of many of these old towns were completely destroyed. Not until 1944 were there bombs of sufficient size and power to penetrate the reinforced concrete of the pens, and in most cases, they still remain, as a memorial to a savage period in sea warfare, and in some cases, as workshops for the present French Navy.

* * *

Turning away from these grisly reminders of the past and after a morning basking — tide permitting — on the wide sandy beach below the walls of the citadel at Port Louis, you might care to lunch

Sea moat, Port Louis

at the *Hôtel Avel Vor*, opposite the port and turn your attention to Breton food.

Brittany is not one of the great gastronomic regions of France and its main claim to culinary fame rests on the variety and excellence of the sea food. A devoted meat-eater would have a rather thin time of it in Brittany. This said, to those who like sea food, are not great gourmets, but nevertheless enjoy good food, Brittany has a great deal to offer.

To begin with, food in Brittany is well cooked, carefully served, plentiful in portions, and relatively inexpensive. Without that, no amount of finger-kissing can save a meal. The over-all standard of cooking is consistently high and I have never had a bad meal there. Bearing in mind the Breton generosity, I have learned to be cautious when ordering a meal, for the portions served can be shattering. A 'starter' of langoustine, when counted, contained twenty three of these giant cray-fish. A plate of *moules farcies*, again when counted, contained eighteen succulent mussels. In each case I had expected around six! So be careful that your eyes are not larger than your capacity, or you may come home looking like a barrel.

Prices are always rising and in a guide book which will stay in print for several years, one should be wary of quoting prices too specifically. However, the standard 4 to 5 course menu currently costs about F.33 (about £4 at the current rate of exchange). One such meal a day is as much as I can take, and this again is usually reserved for the evening, while lunch consists of bread, cheese and fruit on the beach, or in a wayside field.

Sea food is the staple died in Brittany and ranges from little shrimps, scallops and mussels, a variety of oysters from Concarneau, Cancale and the Morbihan, crabs, langoustine, and of course the lobster. That rich dish '*hômard a l'Americaine*' is a Breton dish originally and still in Brittany correctly spelt '*a l'Armorique*'.

Brittany is also very much the country of the *crêpe*, or pancake. These come in two varieties. The buckwheat *galette* is rolled around eggs, ham, cheese or any conceivable savoury filling. A crêperie in Vannes offers a choice of forty different fillings for your *galette*. The *crêpe*, on the other hand, is made from plain wheat and is used as the base for a dessert dish, often with ice-cream. A swift, cheap, snack in a crêperie is the ideal lunch if you are visiting a town centre or want a quick meal when on the road.

Bretons are also very fond of pâtes and pies, which are both rich and inexpensive. Andouillettes, heavy thick sausages, are decidedly an acquired taste, but the *gigot pré-salé*, lamb reared on the salt marshes west of Mont St Michel is really delicious. In St Malo, the sea food platter, *assiette de fruit de mer* is also delicious, but tends to come in enormous portions. I stayed late at one restaurant just to see if the gentleman at a neighbouring table could finish his dish, which consisted of lobster claws, a whole crab, twelve bélon oysters, several langoustines and handfuls of assorted shell fish. When he had polished off the lot — washed down with a bottle of '*Cidre bouché*, the pile of debris on his side-plate was nearly a foot high!

Fish of all kinds is frequently featured either as a soup or a stew. The local version of *bouillabaisse* is called the *cotriade*, and the locals say this is best served at Lomener, a fishing village below Lorient. Trout is good anywhere in the Argoat, while at Châteaulin the salmon is excellent, notably at the *Ducs de Lin*, on the road to Quimper. Breton vegetables are excellent. It has been truly said that one measure of a good cook is the way in which he or she handles vegetables, and by that standard, Breton cooking is excellent indeed.

By the time the time comes, you may be too full for pudding, but apart from the ritual chant "glace — fruit — flan — fromage — tarte-au-chocolate etc." the Bretons have their crêpe and such local dishes as *far*, a sort of sweet custard tart located at the Hotel Roof near Vannes, excellent strawberries from the Plougastel peninsula, and the *quatre-quart* cake, with dried fruit and raisins, which goes very well with coffee.

* * *

On the wine front, it is Muscadet and very little else. Indeed wines from other regions seem distinctly expensive in Breton restaurants, and anyway, Muscadet complements perfectly the sea food you will probably eat at every meal.

Muscadet comes from the *pays Nantais*, the region on the south bank of the Loire west of Nantes, and is a relatively new wine for no one drank Muscadet before the Great War. It is the only wine which takes its name from the grape, rather than the region, like Beaujolais, Bordeaux or Burgundy. Muscadet is a dry, sharp, white wine and naturally complements the local fish and sea food and should be served very cold. Muscadet is best drunk young and, if very young, within three months of the vintage is called *Muscadet-sur-Lie*. In any event it should be drunk within two years, and if you take some bottles home, let it rest before you drink it. *Gros-plant* Muscadet comes from the pays de Retz, again south of the Loire along the Sèvre, and you can buy this wine by the case direct from the growers.

Wine apart, the Bretons drink vast quantities of cider. In the autumn the apple trees which dot the countryside are thick with the small scarlet cider apples, and the smell of apples from the piles in the farmyards is forever wafting in through the car window. Do not be diffident about ordering *cidre* with your meal, for you will quickly notice it on many tables and many Bretons actually prefer it to wine, even to their beloved Muscadet.

* * *

An hour out to sea off Lorient is the island of Groix. This is a steep sided island with a considerable swell smashing against the cliffs even on the calmest day. There is only one port, Port Tudy, on the north shore, and from there it is a short walk across the island to see the great surfing waves foam in at Locmaria bay. The bird life is, as usual, very varied and on the day I was there, the gannets were in

St Cado's

great form, folding their wings high over the sea and plunging deeply into the waves. A visit to Groix takes only half a day and the island is most attractive and, out of season, quite deserted.

Back on the mainland and east of Port Louis lies the chapel of Merlévenez. This is one of the very few Romanesque churches in Brittany and even has those saw-toothed porches typical of the comtemporaneous Norman architecture of England. Merlévenez will make you feel very much at home. Far stranger though is St Cado's, on an island over the estuary of the Etel, although this too is Romanesque and built by the Knights Templar in the very early years of the 12th century.

St Cado was a Welsh saint, who came to Brittany in the 6th century. He eventually left his chapel there to become Bishop of Benevento, but not before he had persuaded the Devil (who must be a very gullible fellow) to help him built the causeway which connects the chapel with the mainland; the deal called for the road to be built in one night and the price was to be the soul of the first across. The Devil anticipated that St Cado himself would make the first trip, but the saint sent his cat across instead. The Devil, no doubt crying "Foiled again!" then decided to breach the causeway, but St Cado booted him into the sea, leaving his saintly footprint on the rocks in the process, where it can still be seen. There is a similar story told in Wales about the Devil's Bridge near Aberystwyth, where one, Blodwin, sent her cow across to pay the Devil's price — and this is the reason why cows have horns! I have no idea if these quaint tales are true, but I think they are amusing and worth recounting. Do visit the little island of St Cado. It is easily missed, but you will not regret going there.

Below St Cado, Etel is a port for tunny fishing which is now a sport as well as an industry, while the estuary above Etel is a sheltered haven for many yachts.

The road south to Quiberon runs past the first of the Morbihan menhirs, near Kerzerho, and you can press on to stay in Plouharnel, and eat at the *Kerank*, or you can turn north to Auray and pass the night at the *Hôtel des Voyageurs*, before we press on again to explore the gulf of Morbihan, the mysteries of the menhirs of Carnac, and the varied islands of the inland sea.

7

Auray, Quiberon and Vannes

Auray is one of the major towns around the Morbihan gulf and it comes as a considerable surprise to discover how small it is. The population barely exceeds eight thousand and it is, in reality, little more than a large village, famous today only for the pilgrim centre at Ste Anne d'Auray to the north and the beautiful *quartier* St Goustan, down by the River Loc.

The way down to the *quartier* is signposted within the town and you should make your first stop down there, on the quai Franklin. Notice first the little Customs House on the Bridge before you stroll down the quai. Here, on 4th December 1776, Benjamin Franklin came ashore, the first ambassador to France from the then rebel colonists of the United States. Franklin's ship had been prevented by foul winds from docking at Nantes and was diverted instead to the port of Auray. The choice of Franklin as ambassador was, in itself, extraordinary for, although he had signed the Declaration of Independence, he was best known in Europe as the inventor of the lightning conductor. This was hardly likely to score many marks at the elegant court of Louis XV, although Louis had watched with fascination when the first lightning conductor was installed in Marly in 1752 and during a storm *"drew sparks from the thunder"*.

However, Franklin went down very well at the French Court and was much admired for his simplicity and honest language, rare virtues in that particular place. He obtained subsidies and arms which enabled the Thirteen Colonies to survive until their victory over Burgoyne at Saratoga brought France openly onto their side.

Opposite the Quai Franklin is the start of the popular Auray

LE 4 DÉCEMBRE 1776
DÉBARQUA À AURAY
BENJAMIN FRANKLIN
ENVOYÉ EN FRANCE
PAR LES ÉTATS-UNIS D'AMÉRIQUE
POUR NÉGOCIER LA PREMIÈRE ALLIANCE
ENTRE LES DEUX PAYS

4 DÉCEMBRE 1926

Franklin plaque, Auray

promenade, which will take you up the hill and give excellent views over Auray and the Morbihan gulf. You will notice, all along the river, the flat oyster platforms of the fishermen, for most of the oysters grown in Brittany are bred from 'spat' cultivated in the Morbihan. You can also take one of the *Vedettes Vertes* boats out of Auray and tour the Gulf.

Heading north towards Ste Anne's you will pass across the marshy flood-plain where, on 29th September 1364 the two rival contenders for the dukedom, Charles of Blois, with Duguesclin and Jean de Montfort with John Chandos, met in their last and decisive battle. Charles was defeated and killed on the field and Duguesclin was captured. Jean was reportedly very upset at the death of his cousin and wept openly until John Chandos pointed out that many men had died to get him the dukedom and the death of his rival was not the greatest loss. Jean later built a chantry chapel and monastery on the battlefield, now the Chartreuse d'Auray, and a memorial to the Chouans.

Ste Anne d'Auray is not a medieval pilgrimage centre. It is still very much alive and the procession there on the 25th July is certainly the most popular *pardon* in Brittany. Ste Anne was the mother of Mary and she has always been a popular saint. The shrine at Auray was established in 1624 when a statue of Ste Anne was unearthed here after a local man, Yves, had a vision and was then led to the site by a ghostly candle, held in an invisible hand. The cult continued to grow for the next two centuries and the present basilica was erected in the 1870s. It is not particularly attractive, although designed to accommodate large numbers of pilgrims, and further chapels are spread over the surrounding park.

You will notice that the roof of the nearby hospital still clearly bears a red cross, painted on it in the last war to warn off hostile aircraft, while a short distance away, and more interesting to my mind, is the memorial on the Champs des Martyrs, which is a memorial to the Chouans shot after the abortive Quiberon battle of 1795.

* * *

The road to Carnac runs south like an arrow from Auray to Plouharnel and brings you quickly to their menhir alignments, focus of all attention in this part of the coast.

A *menhir* is a standing stone and the word derives from the Breton *maen* — stone, and *hir* — long. Although there are menhirs all over France and at many other places in Europe they are most numerous at Carnac. Over 5,000 stones, of varying height, are arranged about the countryside there in long '*alignements*'.

There is nothing aimless about their distribution; they were erected with immense effort and for some definite purpose, but no one knows why or who by. They date certainly from the Neolithic, or New Stone Age, and perhaps the early Bronze Age, and so were there long before the Gauls arrived to found Armorica. Glyn Daniel, a noted British archaeologist, dates them at about 2000 B.C., well before Obelix was on hand to carry them about, but they may be up to 1000 years earlier.

As to their purpose, the field is also wide open. It is generally conceded that their underlying purpose is religious rather than scientific, even though they may have been aligned in a manner which enabled primitive astrologers to fix the date of the Summer

104

Quartier St Goustan, Auray

solstice, or moon-phases, with a view to the correct commencement of religious rites. A recent theory, on the other hand, is that their purpose was entirely scientific, and that they were used for astronomy, though to what use a Neolithic man, even in a society as sophisticated as this, could put such knowledge, even if he had it, has yet to be explained. Whatever their purpose, the menhirs of Carnac are a unique spectacle and draw visitors from all over the world, amazed at their number and the precise way in which they flow away over the fields. Seen on a misty autumn morning, they appear like a frozen army, while by moonlight they are weird indeed.

In Carnac *ville*, just past the High St Michel tumulus is the Prehistorical Museum, established in about 1880 by one James Miln, a Scotsman from Forfar. Miln was a throwback to the earlier age, when amateurism was no barrier to expertise. He began life in the Royal Navy, then became a trader in the East. He studied

105

astonomy, photography and archaeology and spent seven years at Carnac, when, following this last pursuit to its conclusion, he founded the museum. It contains some of the many finds he made during his excavations.

If the purpose of the '*alignements*' is still unexplained, knowledge of the people who erected them is also lacking. Their existence demands a tightly organized society of considerable size and wealth — but who they were and what became of them is still factually unknown, although there is no lack of speculation.

There are three main '*alignements*' at Carnac, and the one at Menec is the biggest and longest, with 1099 menhirs stretching for nearly three quarters of a mile. The other *alignements*, at Kermaria and Kerlescan are smaller, but with higher stones, and plenty of other scattered stones in the fields about.

Before leaving Carnac though, dine at least once at *Chez Maryline* in the main road, where the food and service are unforgettable, or more expensively at the classical *Larn-Roz* in the Avenue de la Poste, or for a good basic meal at *La Bourriche* near the beach. You will find the 'smart' set at La Trinité, nearby.

* * *

You can spend a happy morning among the stone rows of Carnac, before departing south to the 'presqu'ile' de Quiberon.

I like the name *presqu'ile*. In this case it is exactly right, for an 'almost island' is what the Quiberon peninsula has now become. It was originally a true island, but the neck of land has slowly silted up and a causeway through Penthièvre now leads you swiftly across to this most attractive (almost) island.

At Kerhostin you should turn off right on minor roads for the Pointe du Percho, and so down the Côte Sauvage. This is a very rugged coastline and the waves really beat in here in tall combers with spindrift smoking off the top as they thunder in to the beaches and rocks. Be careful where you swim here for the undertows are treacherous. Even fishing can be dangerous, for a sudden extra large wave has snatched many fishermen away from a seemingly secure place on the rocks.

This road will lead you down to the lovely little towns of Port Maria and Quiberon *ville*. You would do well to stay in the Hôtel de La Mer by the port. In the centre of Quiberon you will see the statue

Menhirs, Carnac

to General Hoche, who defeated a 'Chouan' force here in June 1795.

There was, at the time, a civil war in this part of France, between the Catholic pro-Royalist 'Chouans' and the Republican forces under Hoche. A British squadron landed an emigré force from England on Carnac beach, where they were quickly joined by more rebels from the interior, but General Hoche, the Military Governor of Vannes, quickly defeated them. Those who fled and were not speedily evacuated by the British Fleet, were rounded up and shot at Chartreuse, north of Auray. This defeat did serve as some small compensation for the defeat of the French Fleet in Quiberon Bay by Hawke and the capture of Belle Isle by the Royal Marines in 1761, a triumph the Royal Corps still hold as a battle honour. It was to celebrate these successes that David Garrick wrote the 'Hearts of Oak' march for the Royal Navy.

At Port Maria you can take the ferry over to that most famous island, an hour's journey offshore. Belle Isle was only briefly in British hands, for it was exchanged for Nova Scotia in 1763. It had once been owned by Nicolas Fouquet, Chief Minister to the young

Louis XIV. Fouquet had fortified the island in case the King found out about his speculations. He intended to flee there and wait out the storm, but his arrest was too sudden and he lived out his days in the dungeons of Vincennes. His family retained the island until the British arrived, and in the 19th century it became quite fashionable. Sarah Bernhardt had a summer home there on the Pointe des Poulains, and the island is still popular with the famous. It is not too large, about thirty square miles, and the 'Capital', Le Palais, is quite charming. The islands to the east, Houat and Hoedic, are smaller, but can also be visited.

The Quiberon peninsula shelters the Bay from the westerly gales and provides a very large and sheltered anchorage, very popular with yachts. There are also some excellent long sandy beaches popular for "sand" yachting notably by Port Haliguen, and there are more *menhirs* near St Pierre.

Before returning through Auray, go west again across the Crac'h estuary and down to Locmariaquer to see the 'Great Menhir' and the 'Table des Marchands'. The Great Menir was struck by lightning and now lies on the ground, broken into four huge parts. It was once called the *Men-erHroec'h*, the Fairy Wand. The dolmen of the 'Table des Marchands' is a little to the rear and covers a grave. Take note of the carvings on one of the upright stones just inside the entrance.

Locmariaquer is the nearest place to the western shore of the gap

'Table des Marchands', Locmariaquer

through which the sea surges into the Gulf de Morbihan, and you can take a boat from here to tour the Gulf— but be sure it returns here again. If it lands you on the far shore, it's a long walk back.

* * *

The advice on keeping to minor roads has advantages for, if you take the little road south from Auray towards Larmor-Baden to tour around the Gulf, you will come out up on the hill and can look down from there on the little port at Bono, a veritable gem.

From the road bridge above the town you look directly down on the town with the viaduct spanning the river, picked out against the hundreds of white-washed tiles stacked along the quay. These are used to gather the oyster 'spat' and a good point to reflect on the curious sex life of the oyster. Once upon a time oysters bred all round the Breton coast, but ever-increasing pollution and a serious disease has restricted the main breeding ground to the Gulf of Morbihan, from which most oyster embryos come. Brittany has three types of oysters. There is firstly, the huge *Cancale*, from the north coast, about the size of a saucer. Next come the *belons*, which come from Finistère, and lastly the *portugaises*, which come from everywhere but Portugal. None of them contains pearls. The oyster is bi-sexual and self-fertilising, which is rather clever, changing sex from male to female as necessary. Basically, the oyster larvae or 'spat' are first grown on hollow curved tiles, like those you see at Bono. They develop for about six months in shallow water until they are ready to be bedded out in the deeper but richer waters, exposed to the open sea. They stay there for about three years before being cropped, so the oysters you eat are about three-and-a-half to four years old.

If, in spite of all this, you can still cherish an appetite for oysters, then hurry on to the *Hôtel Parc-Fétan*, a Logis de France hotel at Larmor-Baden, with fine views over the Morbihan and out towards the largest of the many islands in the gulf, the Isle aux Moines, 'Monks Island'.

You can get across to the Isle aux Moines from the little port, Port Blanc, above Larmor-Baden, and it lies a bare two hundred metres across the glittering waters. You can cruise all over the gulf in the ferry-boats of the *Vedettes-Vertes* line, and no visit to the Morbihan

109

is complete without a trip on one of their vessels, which you can join at a score of landing stages.

The Gulf of Morbihan covers an area of over 100 square miles, and the sea floods into it between Port Navalo and Kerpenhir, through a gap only six hundred metres wide. The tides and current are, therefore high and fast-flowing, the tidal height being about sixteen feet. There are perhaps scores of islands within the Gulf, some say there is one for every day of the year – it all depends how you define an island. Forty of them are inhabited, of which the largest is the Isle aux Moines. The women of this island are supposed to be remarkably beautiful and are certainly far from ill-favoured. The island once belonged to the religious order, and as it covers an area of 25 square miles it was a considerable fief.

Returning to the mainland you can head north for Vannes, but staying, I suggest, at yet another Logis, the *Hôtel le Roof*, on the little island of Conleau, south of the city, and embarkation point for another major Morbihan island, the Isle d'Arz, before we continue our tour of the Gulf.

*　*　*

Vannes is another place you *must* visit. The old town is a walled city and the walls are ideal, turreted, with machicolations, a real taste of the knightly age. It is best to drive directly down to the harbour and park there, walking up towards the town and the Porte St Vincent, which is dominated by the statue of the Spanish saint, St Vincent Ferrier, who died in the town in 1419. Before you enter his gate, though, bear right, keeping round the walls, for a first spectacular view of the ramparts seen across the formal gardens and the Rohan River which serves the town as a moat.

Walk up towards the Porte Poterne and enter the town that way, looking down to the old houses and *lavoir*, the washing places beneath the gateway, before you enter the cobbled streets of this, the ancient capital of the Breton Kingdom.

This was the home of the *Venetii*, who were defeated by Brutus and then enslaved by Ceasar — their tribal name alone remaining and commemorated at Vannes. In 826 the war-chief Nominöe, became Duke of Brittany, although he was, in all but name, an undisputed sovereign. He gave Brittany the frontiers which it kept until the Revolution of 1789 and he chose Vannes as his capital. The

The Morbihan

city, which gained its cathedral in the 1200's, continued to be the centre for Breton affairs until 1532 when the Estates of Brittany accepted the marriage of Claude of Brittany and François of Angoulême as marking the permanent union of Brittany with the realm of France, so ending the Duchy's existence as a separate power.

Vannes is so full of attractions that it is hard to know where to start. The cathedral of St Pierre stands amid a network of old streets, now free of cars and still lined with leaning, crooked, medieval houses, notably in the Rue de La Monnaie. Note on one, the plump, grinning gargoyles, known as *Vannes and his Wife* and, outside the town hall a fine armoured statue of the Constable de Richemont, brother of Duke John V, and uncle to that unhappy prince, Gilles de Bretagne, whom he tried to protect from his own folly and his brothers wrath. Richemont led the French Army which defeated the English under Talbot at Châtillion in the Dordogne in 1453.

St Pierre is presently in the throes of cleaning and restoration, and is a vast, echoing, gloomy place built as usual in the Flamboyant

111

Cathedral, Vannes

The Walls of Vannes

Gothic style. It contains the tomb of St Vincent, and interesting treasury in the chapter house.

You can eat very well in Vannes at *La Marée Bleue*, and stay, if not at Conleau then at the comfortable *Maréchaudière*, but wherever you stay, see Vannes, for this is a fine city.

* * *

Vannes lies at the head of the Morbihan gulf, and you can reach part of the southern arm of the gulf through Séné, although this road ends at the eastern arm of the gulf. By heading out on the Roche Bernard road and turning off left for Sarzeau, on the Rhuys peninsula, another name with a decidedly Welsh flavour, you will skirt this difficulty and still see the Gulf clearly, away to your right.

This region, once forested, and now very bare, has several interesting sights and the first stop should be at the wonderful moated castle at Suscino. This 13th-century castle was built as a summer

H

Suscino

residence for the Dukes of Brittany. Constable Richemont was born there and Bertrand Duguesclin laid siege to it in 1373 and breached the main curtain wall. The breach can still be identified by the paler stones used to fill it in after the castle was taken, and the English garrison put to the sword. The castle was besieged again during the Wars of Religion and then suffered the usual fate of medieval castles once their day was done, in being gradually dismantled for its supply of dressed stone. Fortunately, this process was halted before it went too far and Suscino — the *Sans-Souci* castle — is now being restored. A walk round the ramparts should only be attempted by those with a head for heights since it is a giddy void on either side, but if this appals, you, then a picnic lunch on the banks of the moat before moving on down the coast, would be a pleasant alternative, or you can cross the main road to Sarzeau itself and dine at the *Hôtel le Sage*.

This is named from the town's most favourite son, Alain-René le Sage, famous as the author of *Gil Blas*. Le Sage was born in 1688 and *Gil Blas*, which is a comedy of manners set in Spain and, to my mind, rather heavy going, is sometimes hailed as the first ever 'modern' French novel. Le Sage was the son of a lawyer and earned his first money as a translator of Spanish books, gaining thereby the background he needed for *Gil Blas*, before he left for Paris and a life of minor fame.

A more enduring name is recalled down the little road to the monastery of St Gildas de Rhuys, where, in about 1136, Abélard, the lover of Héloïse, was appointed as the abbot.

In his time, Abélard enjoyed — and clearly relished — considerable fame as a teacher and a conversationalist. He was himself a Breton, born at La Palet, near Nantes. In 1079 he went to Paris to study at the Schools and quickly came to the attention of his teachers and fellow students, mainly because of his incisive intellect and considerable charm. Abélard questioned, at first gently and then directly, the established doctrines of the Church and since radicals are always popular, at least with the young, he soon attracted a considerable following. He also attracted the attention of one Canon Fulbert, of Notre-Dame, who had a daughter, Héloïse. Héloïse was not only beautiful but extremely intelligent. Fulbert is a much maligned man, but he cannot have been an unthinking brute, for, in an age when women were merely chattels, he had educated Héloïse carefully and he wanted Abélard, the star of Paris, to become her tutor. Abélard moved into the Canon's house and the couple quickly became lovers, but when Héloïse became pregnant, she refused to marry him, leaving him to live with his mother in Brittany and bear a son who was given the unlikely name of Astrolaube. One cannot but suspect that the couple were a trifle precious! Meanwhile, Canon Fulbert was, not without reason, highly incensed. He had invited Paris's leading intellectual into his home where he had promptly debauched his daughter, then failed to marry her, and was now seemingly unrepentant. In the face of his mounting rage, the couple decided to marry, but in secret, which failed to satisfy Canon Fulbert, who wanted his daughter's belated respectability to become widely known, and, finally goaded beyond endurance, he hired some bully-boys who broke into Abélard's lodgings and castrated him!

French farce had turned into tragedy and it is on their subsequent sad lives that the love story of Abélard and Héloïse has been based. The couple parted, Abélard to the Abbey at St Denis and Héloïse

115

into various convents, but they corresponded regularly and their love letters have since become classics. To fill his time and quieten his mind, Abélard then delved even deeper and with increasing dissatisfaction into the doctrines of the Church and in so doing met with increasing opposition. To lie low for a while he accepted the position of Abbot at the remote monastery of St Gildas, but his choice of refuge proved far from happy. The monks were rebellious and far from impressed with his intellect, while the country people were savage and hostile.

"I find myself" wrote Abélard to Héloîse, *"still in danger, a sword forever over my head. I live in a wild country where every day brings new perils."* The monks tried several times to poison him, and he finally fled from the abbey by night and made his way to shelter at Cluny.

His time at St Gildas had not been completely wasted. He established the nunnery at the Paracléte, and installed Héloîse there as abbess, and finally composed his concerns about the Church into a tract, *'Sic-en-Non'* which was published in 1139. The root of Abélard's doubts lay in his opposition to the doctrine of St Anselm *"Through faith shall ye come to understanding."* Abélard, an intelligent man, couldn't accept that and made a counter-proposition, *"I must understand in order that I may believe"* and ran headlong against the disciplines of the Church.

St Bernard of Clairvaux attacked Abélard fiercely and in 1140 brought him before a Council of the Church at Sens where Abélard was roundly condemned. His writings were seized and burned as works tainted with heresy, and only the protection of Peter the Venerable saved him from ending his days in a church prison, *"eating the bred of repentance, and drinking the waters of affliction"* or even at the stake.

Worn out with his life, which had begun so splendidly and was spent in conflict, he returned to Cluny where he died in 1142.

Héloîse lived on until 1163 and died at Paracléte, after which their bodies were brought together at the Père-Lachaise cemetary in Paris *"where, beyond these voices, there is peace"*.

* * *

St Gildas is a small town, dominated by the church and cloisters of the old abbey. It was largely rebuilt in the 17th century, but much of

116

St Gildas

the Romanesque features of Abélard's day still survive, notably in the chancel, and it still contains some interesting objects.

The presbytery contains various relics including the limbs of St Gildas, a Welsh saint who sailed across to Rhuys in the 7th century. His abbey was burned by the Northmen and re-established by St Félix, who built the abbey which Abélard knew. The abbey was the burial place for the ducal family of Brittany should any of them die at Suscino, and several members of the family, notably children, are buried there.

In the summer sun it is hard to find in St Gildas the gloomy spiteful monastery of Abélard's writings, but it can be a bleak spot in winter, when the gales blow in past Belle Isle and sweep the grey town with salty rain.

117

Further on, towards the tip of the peninsula, towards Port Navalo, you will see on the right a tall barrow, the Tumulus of Thumiac from which Caesar is said to have watched Brutus defeat the Venetii. The Venetii were sea-faring folk, with strong, sturdy sailing ships, and Brutus sailed against them in light, oared galleys, taking advantage of a windless day and hurling sickles into the Venetii rigging to bring down their masts. Once the Roman soldiers could board the Venetii ships and fight hand-to-hand, their victory was certain. After the battle all the Venetii warriors were slaughtered and their women and children sold into slavery. From this mount Caesar could see all this coming to pass and if you climb up on top today, there is the sea coast to the south, and to the right, the Gulf of Morbihan laid all before you. Go there at evening and sit on top to watch the sun go down. It sinks slowly and then seems to plunge into the western sky filling the bay with deep purple shadows, while vast flocks of pink-tipped gulls rise from the flooding sand-banks and wheel away to the north.

8

The Eastern Morbihan: Josselin to La Rochebernard

North of Vannes lies rolling country, straddled east and west by the escarpment of the Landes de Lanvaux, which begin near Baud in the west and peter out near Rochefort-en-Terre. This area is frequently described in guidebooks as a moorland, which is why I went there, but it is now intensively cultivated and consists mainly of rich farmland, although the odd patch of ferny heath and rocky outcrop can be found here and there.

A little above Vannes, in a wooded dale you will come to the towers of Elven. These are the remains of a château-fort, built in the 13th century and later owned by the Sieur de Rieux, who was the tutor to Duchesse Anne. The castle was destroyed in 1488 by the troops of Charles VIII, but there are still considerable remains, including the central keep and two gateways. For two years, between 1474 and 1476, it was the prison of Henry Tudor, Duke of Richmond, who later overthrew Richard III on Bosworth Field and became Henry VII of England.

Bear off westwards here, on minor roads and head towards Trédion, on the Lanvaux moors. You will notice that this countryside is dotted with menhirs and megalithic remains while at Trédion, an attractive little place, there is a wide lake fronting a thick walled medieval manor house. This is virtually on the crest of the Lanvaux, with good views to the north and the road dips down now to the valley of the Claie, and leads you north to Guéhenno.

Guéhenno has a calvary, one of the few you will find in the Morbihan. It dates from the mid-16th century, but was restored in the last hundred years. The central cross has two cross-members,

119

and the lower half of the monument carries statues of four apostles. Notice the column in the foreground, which bears the cock which witnessed the denials of Peter.

To the north again, Josselin is one of the most famous towns of Brittany, and seat of the Rohan family.

> *Roi de puis*
> *Prince ne daigne*
> *Rohan suis*

Or, to put it in blunt English:-

> *King I am not*
> *Prince I wouldn't deign to be*
> *I am the Lord de Rohan*

There is so much to see in Josselin that it is hard to know where to start, but since the castle dominates the town, drive down to the River Oust, now canalised, and start from there, where the great castle walls, built on solid rock, rear up high over your head. The river once ran hard against the walls, making Josselin theoretically impregnable, but a road runs there now and from there you get fine views of the castle.

The castle consists of a curtain wall on the river side, dropping downhill at the rear towards the village centre. The castle is still inhabited and remains in the possession of the Rohan family, who have owned it since the Middle Ages.

The original castle was built about 1,000 A.D. by Guéthenoc, Count of Porhoët, and named after his second son, Josselin. Continually modified for the next four hundred years, it withstood, for a while in 1168 a siege by Henry II of England, who was ravaging the lands of those Bretons still resisting the lordship of his son Geoffrey but Henry eventually took the place and destroyed both castle and township. It was rebuilt about 1175 and survived the Hundred Years War, when from 1370 it was held by Oliver de Clisson. His daughter married into the Rohan family and took the castle as her dowry. A dowry was usually a house or land, provided by the bride's family to support their daughter in her old age, when her husband had died and she became a 'dowager'.

The castle was 'slighted', that is, the fortifications were over-thrown, in the 16th century, on the orders of Richelieu, while, during the Revolution the family fled abroad and only returned in 1860 since when much time and money has been spent restoring the

120

The Castle of Josselin

castle, and filling it with antiques and art treasures. It can be visited and one exhibit of particular interest there is the table on which Henri IV signed the Edict of Nantes on the 13th August 1598.

The Rohans, certainly in pre-Revolutionary days, were a very wealthy family with vast estates in France, notably in Anjou, and abroad. Like all old families they have had their share of statesmen and rogues and one son, of a minor branch of the house, in the 18th century, was the Prince de Rohan, a very worldly cleric and cardinal of Strasbourg. De Rohan met Marie-Antoinette and her formidable mother Maria-Theresa when he was appointed Ambassador to the Hapsburg Court at Vienna. His ostentatious dress, gambling and general wildness made a most regrettable impression on the Hapsburg Court and, when Marie-Antoinette became Queen of France, the cardinal's future looked bleak indeed.

De Rohan had a capacity for making unfortunate friends and he had in his train none other than the necromancer and confidence trickster, Cagliostro. No more discreet, the Queen numbered among her ladies, one Jeanne de la Motte, a descendant of the Valois Kings. Now it happened that a Paris jeweller had for sale a necklace valued at the huge sum of one million six hundred thousand livres and, although the Queen refused to let the King buy it for her, saying that for that money they could build a battleship, Cagliostro and Jeanne conspired together to convince the cardinal that she was really desperate to have it and that if he bought the necklace and presented it to the Queen, his future would at once become bright with promise.

The cardinal purchased the necklace and gave it to Jeanne, who, instead of passing it on to the Queen, made off with it. Jeanne broke

Josselin from the River

the necklace up and sold the jewels to shops all over Paris. Some of the diamonds may still be found today at the ears and throats of French nobility. The cardinal, meanwhile, was waiting anxiously for a delighted letter from the Queen and eventually, when it failed to arrive, the whole story came out. The Queen was less than pleased to find her name involved in a confidence trick. The conspirators were caught and, together with the cardinal, flung into the Bastille. After a while and a very brief trial Jeanne was branded and imprisoned; Cagliostro — who had played a very minor role — was censured and deported and the cardinal was banished to the remote and chilling monastery of La Chaise-Dieu in the Auvergne, a long way from the glittering, if doomed, court of the later Bourbons.

* * *

The township of Josselin is small with little more than two thousand people, but a medieval gem, full of leaning timbered houses, and you can walk down the hill of the Rue du Trente on your way to the little chapel of *Notre Dame du Roncier*, 'Our Lady of the Brambles', and you can see them as you pass.

Our Lady of the Brambles has a *pardon* on the second Sunday in September and she is the patroness of epileptics. The shrine dates back to the 15th century when a peasant, cutting back the brambles in his fields, found a statue of the Virgin. He carried it home, but that night it disappeared from his fireside and was found next day once again back among the thorns. This happened several times, until a sanctuary was built on the saint's chosen piece of ground. The original statue, which must have been quite large, was burned by the mob in 1793, but the charred fragment which remains, and a new statue, are still the centre for the annual pilgrimages. The shrine is below ground level and, as it quite usual with Breton shrines, is on the site of a spring.

Back in the town, stands the enormous church of Notre-Dame-du-Roncier, founded in about 1100 and crowned with a great bell-tower. I visited the town on a Sunday when the bells above were going full pelt and the air near the church was almost visibly full of their thunderous clamour. Inside the church is the tomb of Oliver de Clisson, who died at Josselin in 1407 and his wife Marguerite de Rohan, the first châtelaine of the castle.

* * *

Site of the Battle of the Thirty

During one period of the Hundred Years War and during the time of the more local War of the Breton Succession, the seneschal of the castle was the Breton, Jean de Beaumanoir, who held the castle for the Countess of Penthièvre of the Blois faction, and warred with the rival English garrison at nearby Ploërmel, who held their castle for the de Montforts. In March 1351, it being close to Easter and time for the Peace of God, a truce was declared among the rival parties, which did not please Jean de Beaumanoir at all.

On the evening of 26th March, he arrived before the walls of Ploërmel with a herald and, on being admitted, made a startling proposal to the English Knights of the garrison and their leader, Richard Bambro.

He challenged them to meet with the thirty knights of his garrison on the following day at a point mid-way between the two castles and fight to the death with sharpened weapons. His challenge was accepted and the English knights, reinforced by some German men-at-arms to make up the numbers, rode off to the Mi-Voie oak on the following day and met the knights of Josselin. The fight made a great stir in Western Europe and was recounted in Froissart's *Chronicles*. The combatants were all mercenary captains, professional soldiers, and not romatically inclined knight-errants, so both the offer and acceptance were surprising, particularly when, a breach in the knightly code, the Ploërmel faction included some simple men-at-arms in their ranks.

This combat, the *"Combat-de-Trente'*, or Battle of the Thirty, was illegal under the terms of the truce, as it took place during one of those periodic pauses in strife often imposed at the time of religious festivals like Christmas and Easter. Presented as a tournament, it was however widely regarded as an extremely chivalrous encounter and those participants who survived escaped excommunication and gained much glory, although the death role was high and the purpose of the fight was slaughter.

The knights fought on foot, with sword, axe, mace and spear. The fighting went on all day with pauses for refreshment, until the knights were completely exhausted. The Combat finished when a Breton knight mounted and rode his charger through the remaining English knights knocking them to the ground. The outcome was total victory for the Bretons of Blois, eight Englishmen including Bambro being killed, and the rest made prisoner. You will find a vivid account of this fight in Arthur Conan Doyle's historical romance, *Sir Nigel*.

*   *   *

To see the battlefield of the Thirty you must go out towards Ploërmel, past the site and then turn back in the direction of Josselin, for the road is a dual carriageway, and the site cannot be reached from the west-to-east lane. The field is a wide glade surrounded by tall trees and a high obelisk, erected by Louis XVIII dominates the centre of the square. Behind the obelisk is a much smaller and much older cross, where some almost indecipherable carving records the name of Beaumanoir.

The plaque on the main obelisk is a little ironic. It records the names of the Breton Knights, but concludes *"Vive le Roi longtemps, les Bourbons toujours!"* A family, of which it was well said, that they learned nothing and forgot nothing, are now themselves almost forgotten.

Ploërmel is about eight miles from Josselin and a little larger. It was once the seat of the Dukes of Brittany, although their castle, the one from which Bambro marched his men to the Combat, has long since disappeared. There are still traces of the old town walls and in several places they have been converted into the outer wall of houses, high on the ramparts, the gaps in the machicolations, between the merlons, serving as windows.

In the Rue Beaumanoir you will find the Maison des Marmousets, carved with caryatides, and the town has several fine old buildings. The church of St Armel is interesting for the carvings on the doorways, and you should go inside to see the tombs of the two Dukes, Jean II and Jean III. A little way east of Ploermel lies the moated manor at Trécesson, on the edge of Paimpont and the Val-Sans-Retour, but for the moment let us stay in the Morbihan.

You can stay very comfortably near Ploërmel in the *Relais du Val d'Aoust*, at La Chapelle or back in Josselin at the *Hôtel du Chateau*, on the banks of the Oust, and turn your thoughts away from the wars and once again towards food.

* * *

While always good, and frequently excellent, Breton food is sometimes a little predictable. It is firmly based on the produce of the sea and if you spend a long time there, you can feel in need of a change.

Throughout France, as nowhere else in Europe, the variety of the cuisine is remarkable, and it has taken on a new dimension within the last thirty years with the arrival of the Vietnamese from their former colony.

Vietnamese restaurants can be found all over France, and their cooking should not be confused with that of the Chinese. I find Vietnamese food delicious, more delicate and *raffinée* than the Chinese, and served in more sensible portions, although there are some superficial simularities.

All Vietnamese dishes are served in small portions or slices, so that you eat with chopsticks, and even as the French eat everything with bread, and the Belgians eat everything with chips, so all Vietnamese main dishes are served with rice.

A typical Vietnamese meal would begin with soup, or crab-meat,

The 'Argoat'

shrimps, beef, pork or duck, all sliced and mixed with rice or two kinds of noodle, the clear noodle from the soyabean, or rice noodles. If you don't fancy a soup, try a salad with mixed vegetables, mixed again with shrimps, chicken or crab.

Then, a real Vietnamese speciality, try the *Nems*, small crisp spring-rolls, stuffed with pork or crab. These little thumb-size rolls are now very popular in France and quite delicious. Main dishes include *Shop-soy*, sliced meat or shrimps with vegetables; *Mi-xao*, meat with fried noodles; *Canard-Laque*, crisp fried duck; or *Riz Cantonais*, a mixture of rice, ham, shrimps and egg.

These dishes are accompanied by three kinds of sauce, the usual soya bean sauce, a fish sauce, and a very hot pepper-sauce. The dessert is lychees or fruit, and the usual drink is jasmine tea.

I tried my first Vietnamese meal in France from curiosity and boredom, but found it so delicious that a Vietnamese meal is now a regular part of all my travels in France, and in Brittany you may find one a delightful change from seafood.

* * *

128

Turning away south now, towards the coast, you will run back over the Lanvaux 'moors', through Malestroit, down to the town of Rochefort-en-Terre. This is a place I had originally decided to miss, but the road took me there and I am very glad it did, for the little town is full of curious treasures and is, in many ways, quite unique.

It stands on the bluff, overlooking a rocky part of the Lanvaux, and contains the restored 13th-century castle of Rochefort, destroyed by the Catholic League in 1594, again by the Chouans in 1793, and finally rebuilt in the present century. This castle is a private home and can rarely be visited, but do go down and look at the carvings on the postern gate. This is divided into twelve panels showing knights, saints and apostles, and is really quite a work of art, one of those surprising little treasures which can make your day.

The main street, of Grande Rue, which leads back from the castle is full of fine houses, all painted white, and raised up a little above the street level. Notice the hanging signs outside the shops and the carvings on the door panels of the inns and restaurants, a feature of Rochefort-en-Terre.

A little downhill, in a square, lies the church of Notre-Dame-de-la Tronchaye. This is a squat, grey building, with tombs outside the south door, and the nave of the church is below ground level, so that on entering the church, you go down a flight of six steps to reach it.

The statue of Our Lady seems to be very old, a Black Virgin, and is said to date from before the time of the Northmen. It was discovered in a hollow tree (or *tronchaye*) in the 12th century and has a *pardon* on the third Sunday in August. This ornate church is full of late medieval curiosities and well worth a visit. You can eat well in Rochefort at the *Café Breton* and stay at the *Hostellérie du Lion d'Or* in the Grande Rue. If you feel like a stop in really luxurious surroundings then you can travel a little way south to the three-star *Hôtel de Bretagne* at Questembert.

From Rochefort go east, to Redon, not for the town itself, but because it stands on the Vilaine and you can visit the rather fine collections of dolmens, menhirs and megaliths at St Just a little way to the north. This lies, however, outside the Morbihan, in Ille-et-Vilaine, so let us turn south and follow the river, which is the boundary of the *département* of Morbihan, south towards the sea.

At La Roche Bernard they used to build ships. That was back in the 17th century and it has now become little more than a tourist resort and a yachting centre. The town is overlooked by the new, high suspension bridge which carries the main Vannes to Nantes road and gives fine, if giddy, views up the river valley and to the south-east, our first glimpse of the marshland of Brière, our next stop.

Here on the Vilaine, we have to leave the Morbihan and I, for one, do so with considerable regret. It seems to me that it contains all that is best and most interesting in Brittany, a district full of history and colour, with fine food and good weather besides. Still, let us not be despondent, the future is still promising and, after all, we can always come back!

9

Loire-Atlantique: The Brière, Nantes,Châteaubriant

The Vilaine divides the Morbihan from the eastern *département* of Loire-Atlantique and officialdom has widened the breach by detaching the region from Brittany and including it in the new region of 'Pays de la Loire'. We are therefore exaggerating a trifle when we include this area in a book on Brittany.

By decree, therefore, Brittany shrinks, but in reality nothing has changed and, anyway, all this has happened before and with very little effect. Some say that Brittany once extended south, across the Loire, into the Pays de Retz, which most people (myself among them) would include in the Vendée, and Loire-Atlantique began life as Loire-Inférieure, before the Bretons decided that such a title did little for their *amour-propre*, and had it changed.

But enough of these trifles, let us go down into the weird flat-flands of the Brière and travel on through Brittany. The Brière is different, the Camargue of Northern France, a waste of marshes and canals, tall grass and reed beds, lonely, haunting, and strange.

The area lies south, beyond the road between la Roche-Bernard and Nantes, and to get into the heart of the Brière you turn off at the Château de la Bretesche at Missilac, which is quite beatuiful, and head across country on the little roads to la Chapelle-des-Marais and St Joachim.

The word *marais*, or marsh, displays the origins of this country. It was formerly a great bog, a region of sandbanks and salt marsh, now drained by canals but some of the marsh still remains in the very south of the area, around Guérande.

The centre of the Brière is the island of Fédrun and from there, in

131

The Brière

the village, you can take one of the black flat-bottomed punts called *chalands* or *blains*, and pole away along the canals. You won't see much. The grass towers high overhead and the wildlife seems sparse. The scattered houses are mud-walled, whitewashed and heavily thatched, not unlike the cottages you find in the remote parts of Ireland or in the Scottish Highlands. Many are now in ruins, for the native population is withering away and the canals are slowly silting up for lack of use.

For over three hundred years this was the home of a dour and secretive people, who made a bare living, herding sheep, wildfowling, and cutting and selling the peat. The Brière belongs to the residents of the surrounding communities who alone have the right to cut peat there, and then only for a frantic nine days in August. The people and the region have been immortalised in a book by Alphonse de Châteaubriant.

Today many local people have gone to work in the dock-yards at St Nazaire and in 1970 the region was declared a regional park. Since that time it has enjoyed a mild revival, and the increasing income — one can hardly say wealth — of the local people had led to a decline in indiscriminate shooting, so that the population of marsh

132

birds, for which this is a superb habitat, is now on the increase. At Fédrun there is a Park Museum, and an excellent restaurant, the *Auberge du Parc* where the food tries hard to justify the price and almost succeeds.

* * *

The park covers most of a vast headland between the Vilaine and the Loire and you can go south still further through the Porte St Michel and into Guérande. I found Guérande a disappointment, perhaps because it was raining, perhaps because I had expected too much.

It had been described to me as the 'Carcassonne of the North', a fairly serious exaggeration. Guérande is a small walled city, overlooking the grasslands to the north, and the marshlands to the south. You can get a good view of the country from the top of the main gateway, the Porte St Michel, which contains another excellent folklorique museum and, in 1365, saw the signing of the Treaty of Guérande, which healed the breach between the rival claimants to the Duchy and enabled the Dukes to free themsleves from the embrace of the English, and reaffirm their loyalty to France.

The Guérande peninsula is composed of the two arms of Croisic bay, which is slowly silting up and being drained as sheep pasture. Before too many years have passed, it may be possible to drive right round the shore from the point at Piriac-sur-Mer to the Pointe du Croisic. At present, however, you must cross the causeway at Saille and go through Batz, along the coast, past the ruins of many windmills and so into Croisic.

Croisic is a fascinating place. I could live there happily, wandering round the harbour, eating in the many excellent restaurants, notably *Chez Nous* on the *quai* Lenigo, and watching the tide flood in through the narrow gap between the port and Penbron opposite. The town has many fine buildings, dating from the 16th and 17th centuries when the town was an important port. The harbour is divided into three sections, with large colourful trawlers drawn up on the slips and is a great centre for the sardine industry.

The town hall is a maritime museum and this is only proper, for this was the home of Hervé Riel, the pilot who led the French fleet to safety after their defeat in the battle off La Hogue. Riel was a pressed man, and in gratitude for his help and skill, the French admiral,

133

Trawlers, Croisic

Damfreville, offered him any reward he wanted. Riel asked simply
for a short spell of leave to see his wife, Aurore, an event celebrated
by Robert Browning in a rather uneven poem:

> *Name and deed alike are lost,*
> *Not a pillar nor a post,*
> *In his Croisic keeps alive the feat as it befell;*
> *Not a head in white or black,*
> *On a single fishing smack,*
> *In memory of the man but for whom had gone to wrack . . .*

Well, not in Browning's day perhaps, but there is a memorial now
on the Grande Côte and an excessive number of Breton yachts,
fishing boats and small craft seem to be called *La Belle Aurore*.

*   *   *

Along the coast, east of Le Croisic, lies the large and popular resort
of La Baule, like Dinard, its rival on the North Coast, a fashionable

134

spot for the wealthy folk of France and a must for the jaded appetites of *Tout-Paris*.

The beach at La Baule seems to run for miles, well three miles anyway, a multi-coloured parade of red tents and bathers in summer, while yachts and windsurfers cavort in the blue seas beyond. It seems a million miles away from the desolate Brière or the work-a-day folk of Le Croisic.

La Baule is full of fine restaurants and although I prefer the more simple *ambiance* of Le Croisic, you will eat excellently at *l'Espadon* in the Avenue Plage, or less expensively at the *Châlet-Suisse*. Pornichet was once separate from La Baule, but has now been completely absorbed by the larger resort, although it still retains its country market on Wednesdays and Sundays.

If you turn south at Pornichet and go through to the resort of St Marc, it may look familiar and this sense of *déjà-vu* may be explained by the fact that this is where Jacques Tati filmed that classic and hilarious comedy, *Monsieur Hulot's Holiday*.

Back on the coast road to St Nazaire you will pass an obelisk recording the fact that it was through this port which the first American troops of Pershing's Army landed in 1918, while, by the main jetty of the harbour, stands another obelisk, to the fallen of 'Operation Chariot', the great British Commando raid of 1942.

The object of the raid was to destroy the great graving dock, the *Forme Ecluse*, the only dock on the French coast capable of receiving and repairing large German surface raiders.

The force sent against the port consisted of No. 2 Commando and demolition parties from other Commando units, the total raiding party consisting of 285 men. These men were carried in an old American Lease-land exchange destroyer manned by the Royal Navy, *H.M.S. Campbelltown,* and fourteen fast launches.

The bows of *H.M.S. Campbelltown* were crammed with high explosive and the idea was to ram the warship into the lock-gate, land commandos to wreck installations and, after they had withdrawn on the launches, explode the vessel and so destroy the dock.

The force sailed up the river at 10 p.m. on the night of 28th March, flying German ensigns and making suitable signals. They were nearing the docks before their true identity was discovered and the final run was made under heavy fire. The gates were rammed and the commandos landed to destroy much of the dockyard, but this done, withdrawal was impossible. The defences were fully alerted and put

135

St Nazaire

the retreating launches through a gauntlet of fire so that only three managed to return to England. As dawn revealed the chaos at St Nazaire, the German garrison gradually rounded up the surviving commandos and snuffed out pockets of resistance.

Meanwhile, the *'Campbelltown'* remained jammed in the dock gates surrounded by a growing crowd of interested German soldiers, who eventually boarded her. There were nearly four hundred troops there when at noon the ship blew up, destroying the gates and all on board.

The St Nazaire raid was certainly *'the greatest raid of all'*, but the losses were severe. The Royal Navy lost 780 men, and the commandos 212 men out of their total landing force of 265, while many French people were killed in the fighting or in subsequent reprisals.

* * *

Nantes is the largest city in Brittany, the seventh of France, with a population of over a quarter of a million. As a rule I don't like large cities, but Nantes is very agreeable. It has some very necessary sights to see such as the great Castle of the Dukes, some fine museums, scores of good restaurants and hotels, for yet more Breton and Vietnamese food, and in the large network of pedestrian precincts, all the best shopping of France.

Nantes is a very ancient city, a capital of the Gaulish tribe, the *Namnetes*, hence Nantes, and was later a trading centre for the Romans. During the time of the Dukes and indeed right up until the time when this *département* was detached from the province, Nantes and Rennes debated their claims to be the capital of Brittany, and Nantes for size and style has to be declared the winner.

The castle was begun by Duke Francois II and completed by Duchesse Anne. It greatly impressed Henri IV when he arrived in the city and it was here that he signed the Edict of Nantes which granted religious toleration to the Protestants and ended, for a while anyway, the Wars of Religion.

To visit Nantes, drive into the centre and park near the castle, off the Rue Henri IV. The main part of the city lies to the west, along the Cours Franklin Roosevelt, but the two great attractions of castle and cathedral are just to hand and may be visited within the morning, while from here the best way to see the city, or indeed any city, is to walk.

Nantes has always been a port and was once a slaving centre –

The great Château, Nantes

cloth to Africa, slaves to the West Indies, with rum, sugar and spices on the return voyage. The slave merchants' houses still stand in the old part of the town, close to the river-port facilities, and built from vast profits, very fine houses they are.

* * *

Like most castles, the one in Nantes has had its ups and downs, serving as a palace, garrison and prison. Fouquet was arrested here and 'Bluebeard' Gilles de Rais was tried for his crimes in the castle hall and burned at the stake on the river bank nearby. Gilles had been a great soldier. He rode with Joan of Arc and became Marshal of France, but he was more than a little mad and after returning to his estates in the Vendée, he turned to witchcraft, necromancy and mass-murder, slaughtering children by the dozen, searching for the elixir of life, before he was finally arrested. The castle of Nantes is moated, and the walls are tall. Inside is an excellent museum of Breton costume and furniture, including some fine *lit-clos*, and a maritime museum with relics of the slave trade.

From the castle it is a short walk to the cathedral of St Pierre. Do not be disappointed by the exterior, which is, in any case, being restored. Go inside and wonder. The cathedral was built from about 1400, of limestone, not in the usual granite, a soaring example of the Flamboyant Gothic, but with more than a touch of the pleasing Perpendicular. The vault of the nave is 120 ft. above you and the clean lines of the pillars seem to make it far higher than that. The roof was destroyed by fire in 1972 and the restoration work is still in progress, but the interior is in excellent condition and uncluttered by excessive ornamentation. In one corner is the tomb of Duke Francois II and his wife Margarite of Foix. The side-niches of the tomb contain exquisite statues or 'weepers', including saints and martyrs and, most unusually, one of St Charlemagne, who was not even a cleric and by no means a saint.

All this part of the town is worth exploring, and a little way along the Rue Clemenceau you will come to the Musée des Beaux Arts, one of the finest provincial art galleries in France. There are eighteen galleries with works by masters of all the periods, notably by Georges de la Tour and portraits by Ingres. The Spanish collection is particularly fine.

You can return to the centre of the town and pass through the

138

botanical gardens, which has a statue of Jules Verne, who was born in Nantes, before wandering through the narrow streets around the area of *Au Bon Vieux Temps*.

There is nothing to do here but wander about window-shopping, but if you circle the exquisite Place Royale, with its fountain, you will come to the Cours Cambronne, with the statue of yet another prominent *Nantais,* General Cambronne, who commanded the infantry of the Old Guard at Waterloo and sprang into the history books on the strength of one forceful phrase. Exactly what the phrase was is still disputed.

The delicate and romantic say that, when summoned to surrender by the English he replied *"La Garde meurt mais ne se rend pas"* best translated as "The Guard knows how to die but not how to surrender". The more prosaic believe he retorted simply *'Merde!'* The first remark sounds like the sort one would have wished to say, but thought of later, while the second is far more likely, and considerably more soldierly.

Nantes is fairly rich in native sons for, apart from Jules Verne and Cambronne, we have Waldeck-Rousseau, the longest reigning prime-minister of the Third Republic, Lamoricière, General of the Algerian wars who captured the Riff leader Abd-el-Kader, another notable prime-minister, Briand, and, over the ages, assorted dukes and princes.

* * *

If you continue past the Cours Cambronne down to the riverine port, you will see many interesting sights, and some fine old buildings, especially along the quai de la Fosse. Number 70 was once the capital of the French East India Company, while many of the others belonged to merchants who grew regrettably rich from the profits of the slave trade. Their houses can be distinguished by their elegant wrought-iron decoration on the window grilles and gates.

From the Place l'Herminer up to the Place Graslin, where at No. 3 Cambronne died in 1842, are many little shops and restaurants, for Nantes food is famous and very varied. *La Cigogne* in the Rue Jean-Jacques Rousseau is excellent, and you can get away from the inevitable fish at *Les Maraichers* in the Rue Fouré, and there are many other excellent restaurants in the country round about.

* * *

From Nantes, the traveller has a choice. He can return to St Nazaire to cross the Loire by the spectacular new bridge and visit the lands of the *pays de Retz*, or travel up the river, through the Muscadet country to the frontier of Brittany at Ancenis or finally, head north along the valley of the Erdre towards Châteaubriant, and so out of Loire-Atlantique altogether and into the Ile-et-Vilaine.

Each has its advantages and although now out of Brittany completely, the *pays de Retz* can hardly be ignored. It has some fine resorts, notably Pornic on the so-called Jade Coast, and the interesting island of Noirmoutier, where St Philibert established his mission to the savage pagan Gauls, returning through Machecoul, capital of the *pays de Retz*, with the donjon of Gilles de Rais' sinister castle. Inland you should see the great castle at Clisson on the Sèvre. This was largely destroyed, with the rest of the town in 1794, but the elements which remain are imposing and picturesque.

North of Clisson, along the Sèvre, is the Muscadet country proper, and a chance to purchase a case or two directly from the *vignerons* before you run up to Champtoceaux and Ancenis.

You can eat very well at the *Voyageurs* in Champtoceaux, walking off the effects afterwards by strolling along the promenade de Champalud.

From Nantes a river trip up the Erdre is a favourite Sunday excursion for the *nantais* and the pleasure-craft are moored in rows along the banks north of the town. If you travel by car, it is as well to leave the camion-infested N.37 as soon as possible and travel instead by the minor roads from La Chapelle-sur-Erdre through Sucé, across the Nantes-Brest canal and so to North. From here it is a pleasant run up to our last call in this *département*, the town of Châteaubriant.

Châteaubriant is in some ways a sad place. It is dominated by a huge castle, the ancestral home of the Lavals. When one Lord of Laval returned to his castle from the Crusades, his wife was so pleased to see him she expired in his arms, which must have given that doughty knight quite a nasty turn, but the later history is even less attractive. In the 16th century, the then Count Jean, married the beautiful Françoise de Foix and, knowing the King's reputation with the ladies, left his wife at home when summoned to court by François the First.

The King heard of the Count's beautiful wife, but when the Count declined to produce her he discovered a signal by which the Count

General Cambronne, Nantes

Execution ground, Châteaubriant

could summon the lady. The King sent off the signal himself and to
the Count's rage, his wife duly appeared at court. Had the Count
stayed with his wife all might have been well, but he stormed off
home to Châteaubriant and left her behind and she eventually
became the King's mistress.

When the King tired of her, she went home to Châteaubriant,
where the Count kept her and her daughter imprisoned in a dar-
kened room for ten years. The daughter died and, in the end, the
Count murdered his wife. She must have been a most unhappy lady.

In the last war (there is more of this I'm afraid), there was a prison
camp outside Châteaubriant, used to confine suspected Resistance
men, and hostages taken by the Germans and held against the good
behaviour of the populace.

Unfortunately, in October 1941, Colonel Holtz, commander of
the garrison at Nantes, was ambushed and killed. As a reprisal,
twenty-five men, some old, one only sixteen, were taken from the
camp to a small quarry west of the town and shot. A further
twenty-one were taken to Nantes and shot there.

The execution site has become a place of pilgrimage, with a stark memorial dominating the execution posts and studded with urns containing earth sent from every province of France by Maquis *réseau* as well as from the various concentration camps of the Third Reich. There is nothing even remotely beautiful about this scene. It is a terrible place.

Châteaubriant *ville* is dominated by the great castle of the Counts. Like most castles it was pulled down or remodelled several times and now largely dates from the late Renaissance. The keep is all that remains of the original medieval fortress and the buildings now contain a museum, the law courts, and the municipal offices.

The castle is imposing but the town seems depressed, so from Châteaubriant it is now north again for Rennes, to the present capitcal of the Province, and a visit to the frontier towns of the grand old Duchy.

10

Ille et Vilaine: Brocélainde, Rennes, Fougères

The north-eastern *département* of Ille et Vilaine, full of interest and variety, contains many of the real gems the traveller seeks in the Breton countryside. This is truly a *département* crammed with curiosities and to start on a high note, you should travel west from Châteaubriant, almost to the borders of Morbihan, to the ancient and legendary forest of Brocéliande.

You will not find Brocéliande on any modern map. Today it is known as the forest of Paimpont, and echoes to the screech of saws and the crash of falling timber, but this, be aware, is a forest of romance and mystery, recognised as such for over two thousand years, and a place to approach with caution.

Brocéliande is the classic example of how, in Brittany, fact and legend are inextricably mixed. On the face of it, this is just a forest, one of those great medieval hunting grounds and preserved as such since ancient times.

However, this particular forest has gathered a great mass of legendary stories, appeared in ancient plays and chanson de geste, and offered magical potential from Druidic times to the present day; and to tell this story, where shall we begin?

Let us start with King Arthur or, to be more exact, with Merlin, his mentor and wizard, who came to a sticky end among these green acres. Merlin, who here appears as a young man, rather than an old warlock with pointed hat and beard, was loved by the fairy Viviane, the Lady of the Lake who was born in the château of Comper. Viviane, who had met King Arthur's knights before, was afraid of losing Merlin, so she cast a spell upon him and, while he slept,

144

The Fountain of Baranton

encased him forever — some say inside an oak, others, inside a stone. Some say — and even believe — that Merlin is still there, in the *Val sans Retour*, the Valley of No Return, near Trécesson, or that he is inside the Merlin stone by the spring at Baranton.

To find the spring at Baranton is far from easy. Concoret is the largest place nearby and from there you travel through la Saudrais and turn off to the curiously named hamlet of Folle-Pensée.

At the far end of the village a sign points into the woods stating positively, '*Fontaine de Baranton*'. The path is initially wide, then narrows, then dwindles, and finally disappears. Head south-west, on gradually rising ground and you *may* come to a place where small stones and rocks mark the route of an ancient path. Follow this for a while and suddenly, in a grove of oak trees, you will come to the fairy spring.

It is contained in a deep granite basin, clear and cold water with a metellic taste. At the head of the basin, cast aside, and resembling an extra large kerb-stone, is the *perron de Merlin*, which is said on good historical evidence to have magic powers.

K

To summon rain you take some water from the spring, sprinkle it on the stone and, within the hour, clouds gather and the rain and hail comes down. This belief certainly dates from Druidic times, and processions came to the spring and invoked its aid as recently as 1935. In 1835, during a severe drought, the Vicar of Concoret led his congregation there, blessed the water and sprinkled it on the stone, at which *"a violent thunderstorm arose and the rain fell with such violence that we hastened to disperse."*

These are just two of the legends of Brocéliande, but you will find more cropping up again and again, in the old Arthurian legends and subsequent folklore. Here, King Arthur's knights searched for the Holy Grail and here, Morgan le Fay, or *Fée*, the fairy, wove her plots.

The legend of Baranton's spring was certainly in existence as long ago as the 5th century and repeated almost exactly in Wace's *Roman de Rou*, which was written in about 1100.

Now, is it all true? Personally, I have no idea, but let Wace have the last word on it:

> *Not all lies, not all truth,*
> *Not all fable, not all sooth.*

Two final points: Getting to the fountain was difficult; getting back proved almost impossible. I got gloriously lost and had I not stumbled across a forester who led me out, I might be wandering there yet. When I told him that I had searched for the fountain and found it, he was amazed, "You are very lucky" he said, "very few people have seen it." Footsore and covered in mud, I didn't *feel* very lucky.

Finally, you will be wondering, did I sprinkle water on the stone and did it work? I did, and it didn't. I don't know whether I'm pleased about that or not, but I do know that the forest of Brocéliande is a very strange place.

*   *   *

Stamping about in the woods always gives me an appetite and after this particular wood, an added incentive for human company and good food. East then to Rennes, to stay at the *Du Guesclin* by the station, and dine at *Le Corsaire*, where I recounted my adventures to an interested waiter.

Rue St Georges, Rennes

Since Nantes has departed to join the Pays de La Loire, Rennes is the undoubted capital of Brittany. Even without this defection, Rennes has all the attributes of a capital, a University, a Palais de Justice, where the unfortunate Dreyfus was tried for the second time in 1899, and some fine public buildings. The nightlife is conspicuous by its absence, but the restaurants and hotels are very good so that, as a centre for touring Ille-et-Vilaine, Rennes has much commend it.

The city is divided in two by the Vilaine and is hell for the driver, so it is as well to abandon your car at the station, give your hotel porter enough money to keep the meter fed, and explore the town on foot.

The old *quartier* of the town, which is always the most attractive part in any town, is now the usual pedestrian precinct and lies south of the Palais du Commerce. The Rue St Georges is full of fine houses and has one good restaurant, *Le Baron*. I was taking photographs in this street when an elderly gentleman took me by the arm and insisted on showing me the courtyards which lie behind these façades. Each house has its interior courtyard, and you should probe up these narrow alleyways to see what lies behind.

The cathedral of St Pierre is a massive place, and towers over the Place des Lices, the ancient lists or tournament ground, where Bertrand Duguesclin made his anonymous debut in 1337, overthrowing one knight after another. He was so poor at the time that he had to borrow armour from one of his cousins and wearing borrowed armour was horribly uncomfortable, but in spite of this Bertrand triumphed. Finally, Bertrand's visor was knocked open and his father, who had until then been more than a little ashamed of his ugly little son, rushed down to pound him on the back and promise him the finest mail that money could buy.

The medieval town was largely destroyed in the great fire of 1720 when the town burned for several days. The rebuilding was done on classical lines and the centre of the town is most attractive.

The Law Courts are a very ancient foundation. Rennes has been the seat of the *Parlement* of Brittany since the days of the Duchesse Anne, and consistently maintained the rights of the duchy against the encroachments of King and Paris. Much of this power has now vanished, but the magnificent council chambers remain, and can be visited. Like all good capitals, Rennes has art galleries, concert halls, and an active artistic and social life, largely centred on the

148

University. The townspeople will tell you that for fun and frolic, Rennes leaves much to be desired, but as a touring centre for the visitor it is ideal.

* * *

To the west lies the frontier and the dread land of France. Guarding the approaches, therefore, is a series of fortified towns and no traveller to Brittany should fail to visit the greatest fortresses of all at Vitré and Fougères.

Vitré, to the south, is the nearest and can be reached after side visits to the ruins at Châteaugiron, and the Fairy's Rock near La Guerche-de-Bretagne.

Vitré leaps at you, especially if you come in down the hill from the south. You will round the corner and are confronted with the old houses, the walls, the medieval gateways, and the cobbled narrow streets leading up into the old town. The château-fort ramparts are huge, with a deep moat, spanned by a drawbridge. It dates from the Hundred Years War, fell into ruin and was purchased by the municipality in 1820 for a mere 8,000 francs.

You can get a good view of the castle from the banks of the little garden opposite the Rue d'Embas. Off this lies the Rue Beaudrairie, very medieval, and this will lead you uphill to the courtyard facing the castle.

Below the north wall lies the suburb of La Rachapt. This was seized by English *routiers*, freebooters, during the Hundred Years War and, although the castle remained in French hands, the garrison felt uneasy with those perfidious *anglais* loafing about beneath their feet, so they eventually levied a large enough bribe from the townspeople to tempt the English to march away. Rechapt is a corruption of the word *rechat*, to 're-purchase'. This suburb later became a hotbed of Calvinism during the Wars of Religion when the town belonged to the unfortunate Coligny family.

The streets of the town are full of interest and on one wall of the church of Notre Dame, please notice the outside pulpit, used firstly to preach to the townsfolk and later, in Coligny's day, by the Catholic priests to argue doctrinal points with Protestant pastors in the house opposite. Vitré is a fine place, certainly one of the most interesting towns of France for the medievalist, and, on the road north, stop on the *Tertres Noirs*, a small hill just outside the town

Castle and walls of Vitré

and look back from there. As the sun goes down the walls and shadows of Vitré look black and formidable against the sky.

* * *

Fougères grows on you. This is the Breton town which appears on all the posters, so that when you arrive, and are carried into the town on a tidal wave of traffic, it can be a little alarming.

However, it improves. The pearl of Fougères is not the town, but the castle, and this lies below and beyond the town itself. Some castle-builders preferred hill sites, but others preferred the valleys where they could divert some river into an impassable moat, and so it is with Fourgères. A walk round the walls of the castle reveals military architecture at its finest. There are high walls built on rock and screened by the moat. Getting over these walls, even today, unopposed, would be a task indeed. In fact, although the town on

150

the hill is one of those places which Hitler knocked about a bit, the castle has survived seven hundred years of conflict remarkably well.

The first castle on this site was built before the Conquest, but it fell to Henry II Plantagenet, in 1166, when he was invading the Duchy to advance the claims of his son Geoffrey and Henry levelled this castle to the ground. The present castle was begun shortly afterwards, although the first of the present towers was only erected in the 14th century. The castle was besieged incessantly during the Hundred Years War and changed hands several times. The best view of the castle is offered from the lower water gate, near the castle mill and from here the castle runs off, along the spur, and encloses a large parkland. You can visit the castle and walk along the ramparts inside, looking out on town and *bourg*, a really evocative way to visit this doughty fortress.

Fourgères *ville* is less inspiring, but quite agreeable. You can get a good view over the castle from the public gardens, the Place des Arbres, while the *Lion d'Or* is a good place to stay, especially if you dine at the *Restaurant St Pierre* next door.

* * *

To stay strictly within the boundaries of the province, you should head east from Fougères for Tramblay, but here my courage failed me and I turned north for a visit to the island monastery at Mont St Michel. In fact, this is an excusable diversion, because whether Mont St Michel lies in Brittany or Normandy, depends entirely on the course of the River Couesnon, which historically marks the frontier between the two great duchies and runs about the island. The river, backed up along its course by the fierce tides of the bay has changed course frequently and now places this spectacular site firmly in Normandy, but only just.

I have visited Mont St Michel several times and would advise you, if possible, to visit it out of season, preferably in the early spring or late autumn. This last time was in November on a grey cold day, when the normally crowded streets were empty and even Mère Poulard's restaurant was taking its annual *congé*. A chill wind swept round every corner and the monastery, quite deserted, seemed almost haunted. I managed to get lost again here and wandered around for a long while, heaving open heavy oak doors and climbing up and down endless flights of steps until I thankfully emerged on the great terrance and out into a howling gale.

151

From this windy platform, the bay below was spectacular, the tide sweeping in with a series of tall waves, crashing over into foam and white crests. They say that the tide sweeps into St Michel's bay at the speed of a galloping horse and that day it was a fearsome sight, even from my safe vantage point 300 feet above the waves.

The abbey was begun in the 8th century and dedicated to the

Mont St Michel

Archangel Michel, who fought a duel with the devil on nearby Mont Dol and afterwards directed the Bishop of Avranches to build a chantry chapel on the lonely island in the bay to keep the devil away. This chapel, much altered, still stands as a place of pilgrimage and now contains a large silver statue of the saint.

In later centuries the island became a monastery, a fortress and a prison and eventually, given the glorious site, a tourist trap. It cannot be missed though, and no visitor should leave without visiting the *Restaurant de La Mère Poulard*, and having one of their huge feathery omelettes. These are large dishes, each as big as a soup plate, frothing inside and puffing jets of steam as the waiter slides it on to your plate. Mont St Michel is a necessary visit, in or out of season, but you should try and arrive at sunset, when the westering sun sweeps down out of the sky and fills the bay with shadows.

Then you can regain the mainland by the causeway and dine very comfortably at the *Hôtel au Bon Accueil* on the road to Pontorson.

* * *

Our road lies to the west now, on the last lap back to St Malo and the Ferry home, but Brittany has a strong grip and will not willingly let you go. You can, if you have time to spare, walk down the Valley of the Cousenon, on that entrancing footpath, the GR.39, which leads south, past Tramblay and eventually, after some sixty miles, to the capital at Rennes, or stroll into Normandy along the coast for Brittany is full of footpaths, especially those waymarked trails of the *Comité National des Sentiers de Grande Randonneé* and, with plenty of campsites available for overnight stops, the whole province is a walker's paradise in whatever area you choose to roam.

We must go west though, across the reclaimed 'polders' around Mont St Michel, and so to Mont Dol, and the nearby town of Dol-de-Bretagne. Mont Dol, which dominates this flat hinterland was once, like Mont St Michel, an island. It is a granite knoll, some 200 feet in height and now a pilgrim centre, a mixture of little chapels and ruined windmills.

You can see Mont St Michel from Mont Dol and inspect, stamped in the rock there, the footprints of St Michel, for it is here that he fought hand in hand with the Devil. Before the fight St Michel was on his Mount out in the bay and leapt across to Mont Dol to accept the Devil's challenge. Some people will believe anything!

The land between the two islands has been steadily drained since the 13th century and is now much used as grazing land for sheep. They provide the basis for that delicious tangy mutton, from the *pré-salé*, the salt-fields. Dol itself is a little place with the usual quaint collection of old houses and at least one excellent restaurant the *Bretagne*.

South of Dol lies the great castle at Combourg, home of René de Châteaubriant and this large and gloomy castle provided some of the grimmer passages in his *Mémoires d'Outre-Tombe*. At the time the family lived there money was in short supply and René spent much of his time in his draughty bedroom, plagued by fears of ghosts and listening fearfully to the wind moaning round the towers. Even today, Combourg, swathed in tall trees is hardly a jaunty castle, but it is admittedly imposing, especially when seem from across the park, if you go north on the minor road towards Cancale.

Cancale is an oyster port. No, let me re-state that; Cancale is *the* oyster port, and a very attractive place to visit. This is the gateway to the *Côte d'Emeraude*, and solely devoted to the oyster, growing garnering and eating them in vast amounts.

The Castle of Fougères

The oyster beds lie out in the bay and scores of boats go out at each ebb, 'Springs', to gather in the harvest. Most of the catch is cleaned and consumed in the hotels and restaurants behind the beach. The bay contains the three main types of oyster, the large *cancales*, the *bélons*, and the little *portugaises*. Personally, I like the bélon, but for a sea food feast, do not leave before eating at least once at *Le Cancalais* on the quai Gambetta.

On your final run, go out to the Pointe du Grouin, and follow the *corniche* route along the coast, for even here, at the last minute, the duchy will surprise you with still more secret coves and sudden stretches of golden sands swept by the green sea, before you come through Rotheneuf, and the hotels of Paramé, and so into the town of St Malo.

Something should always be kept for the end, and dinner at *L'Abordage* in the Place de la Poissonnerie, will keep your spirits up on the final evening, until, with the following day, the bright ferry comes round the Grande Bé, and takes you back again to your island.

Bibliography

Brittany by Henry Myhill — Faber & Faber 1964
Early Brittany by Nora Chadwick — University of Wales Press 1969
Oyster River by George Millar — Bodley Head 1963
Brittany by A.H. Broderick — Hodder & Stoughton 1951
Brittany and the Bretons by Keith Spence — Gollancz 1978
Brittany Roundabout by Garry Hogg — Museum Press 1953
La Bretagne et du Maine — Total Guide 1975
Gault Millau Guide de La France (current edition)
Brittany — Michelin Green Guide 1974
Guide Michelin 1978
Guide des Auberges et Logis de France (current edition)
Brittany by Brian Jackman and Margaret Hides — Sunday Times 1975
The Devil's Brood by Alfred Duggan — Transworld 1977
Ducal Brittany 1364-1399 by Michael Jones — OUP 1970

Index